BERGGASSE 19

BERGGASSE 19

Sigmund Freud's Home

THE PHOTOGRAPHS OF

WITH AN INTRODUCTION BY PETER GAY

CAPTIONS BY RITA RANSOHOFF

and Offices, Vienna 1938

Edmund Engelman

Basic Books, Inc., Publishers   New York

Library of Congress Cataloging in Publication Data

Engelman, Edmund, 1907–
    Berggasse 19.

    Includes bibliography
    1.   Freud, Sigmund, 1856-1939—Homes and haunts—
Pictorial works.   I.   Title.
BF173.F85E6   150'.19'520924 [B]   76-45652
ISBN: 0–465–00656–6

Introduction: Freud/"For the Marble Tablet," copyright © 1976
by Peter Gay.
Captions to the photographs, copyright © 1976 by Basic Books, Inc.
The photographs of Berggasse 19, copyright © 1976
by Edmund Engelman.
A Memoir, copyright © 1976 by Edmund Engelman.
Library of Congress Card Number: 76–7686
ISBN: 0–465–0065606
Printed in the United States of America
Designed by Vincent Torre
76 77 78 79 80   10 9 8 7 6 5 4 3 2 1

TO IRENE

CONTENTS

BERGGASSE 19

INTRODUCTION

Freud
For the Marble Tablet

BY PETER GAY

AFTER I had lived with the Frankels several weeks [in 1921], the old Mr. Frankel thought it was part of his duty as a host to come and ask me how I was enjoying my sojourn in Vienna. He asked, "What are you doing here?" And I told him I was studying with Professor Freud. He said: "Professor Freud? Never heard the name." And he added: "Moreover, I should know, because my son-in-law is a professor at the University, and I know all the professors in the University of Vienna. But on the other hand, that name does sound familiar." Then he disappeared for a minute or two and came back with a little book, the pages of which he was fumbling and reading down the line: "F, F, F, Freud, Freud, here he is, Freud, Sigmund, Berggasse 19, a lodge brother of mine!" Mr. Frankel was reading from the Vienna catalogue of the members of the B'nai B'rith Abraham. When I told Freud this story, he was greatly amused. "You see," he said, "a prophet is never known in his own country."

—Abraham Kardiner, *"Freud—The Man I Knew,*
The Scientist, and His Influence"

BERGGASSE 19, where Sigmund Freud lived for nearly half a century, is an unpretentious apartment house on a respectable residential street in northern Vienna. When he moved there in the summer of 1891 to take a small apartment, Freud was a promising young neurologist with unorthodox ideas and a future to make; when he left the house and Nazi-occupied Austria in June 1938 "to die in freedom,"[1] he was a world-famous old man, founder of a science as pervasive in its influence as it was controversial in its claims. He enacted much quiet drama in this building; the silent struggles and private triumphs that mark the lives of all intellectual innovators marked this innovator more than others. Here, at Berggasse 19, Freud wrote most of his books and analyzed most of his patients, including the first and most historic of all his analysands, himself; here he gathered his library, collected his art, met his associates, raised his children, and conducted a voluminous correspondence in which he rehearsed his momentous ideas and kept the threads of the psychoanalytic movement from twisting or from disintegrating altogether. His apartment is now a museum, and a plaque informs the passer-by that Sigmund Freud "lived and worked" here. The celebration seems modest enough for one of the decisive discoverers in history, for the Columbus of the mind. Nor does the plaque represent an effusion of local pride: it was put up in 1953 by the World Federation for Mental Health. In fact, most of the recognition Freud has received in Vienna has been the work of foreigners: his bust, which now stands in the University, was presented by Ernest Jones. There is in Vienna, crisscrossed with streets named after its great, or at least prominent, residents, no Freudgasse.[2] Guidebooks and leaflets advertising the city, though in their accustomed way assiduous in rescuing once-famous Viennese from oblivion, barely mention his name. The public indifference, the latent hostility, are chilling. Freud, the first psychologist to chart the workings of ambivalence, had, in this city he hated but could not leave, abundant materials for the exercise of mixed feelings. Vienna, it seems, has largely repressed Freud.

But Freud is irrepressible. He has scattered rich and rewarding clues to himself, to his way of thinking and his mode of working, to his habits and his aversions. His autobiographical writings are terse but informative. His letters are abundant, energetic, and wholly unmistakable. Best of all, his scientific works provide sketch maps to his innermost nature. Considering the kind of science he founded, they could not do anything less: psychoanalysis is controlled and deep autobiography, and as the first psychoanalyst, compelled as he was to use himself as material, Freud found it necessary to publish some of his most private fantasies. His life was among his best documents.

Yet Freud presents himself to the world not without masks—some of them deliberate strategies of self-protection, others unconscious devices. It is true, and helpful, that Freud was not afflicted with the vice of modesty. He spoke and wrote of his discoveries and accomplishments with an engaging absence of coyness; as a well-loved

14

child, he had a firm sense of his gifts. But he failed, for all his confidence, to recognize the full measure of his qualities and of his historic stature. In a famous autobiographical summing up, he told his friend Wilhelm Fliess in February 1900, "I am actually not a man of science at all, not an observer, not an experimenter, not a thinker. I am nothing but a conquistador by temperament, an adventurer, if you want to translate this term, with all the inquisitiveness, daring and tenacity of such a man."[3] The passage is candid and sincere. Fliess was a prominent ear, nose, and throat specialist with a lucrative practice in Berlin, a man of charismatic presence and with scientific ambitions second only to Freud's own; during the 1890s, the lonely decade of Freud's discoveries, he was Freud's closest friend, indeed his only friend. But while we may accept Freud's denials as a serious attempt at self-appraisal, we must reject its pretensions to being an accurate self-portrait. It suggests the solidity of his self-regard, the strength of his ego; it exemplifies his readiness to speak of himself with large, sweeping gestures. But it displays, too, a certain myopia, and a reductionism rare in Freud's thinking. Freud was in many respects unique, but in this he was like other humans: he was not his own best judge.

His misjudgment, coupled as it was with a fierce desire to guard his privacy, has generated a contradiction which every student of Freud must confront. Freud's science was, above all, the science of candor. The technique of psychoanalysis depends, as everyone knows, on the uninhibited freedom with which the analysand produces his associations, without fear and without reserve; his most illogical notions and most forbidden desires must come out, and be recorded, in the apparent disorder in which they emerge into his awareness. He must arrange nothing, conceal nothing: the psychoanalyst and the censor are sworn enemies. The candor is, to be sure, one-sided; Freud said more than once that for the sake of the patient the psychoanalyst must remain a stranger, keeping himself to himself, a blank sheet on which the analysand inscribes his transferences. But Freud stands in history as analyst and as analysand, and we must see him in both capacities to see him at all, as Freud himself did in the course of his self-analysis. Yet here he fails his historian, at least partially. His confessions in *The Interpretation of Dreams* and elsewhere, intimate and copious as they are, require elucidation, enlargement, correction—in short, interpretation. They often sound grudging, almost extorted. Max Schur, Freud's physician and friend, notes the reluctance with which

Goethe, and on Freud himself, for centuries. "A basket of orchids," he told Fliess on the occasion of his forty-fifth birthday, "shams splendor and the blazing sun, a piece of a Pompeiian wall with a centaur and faun translates me to longed-for Italy."[8] Collecting was for Freud the passion of his life: Max Schur records that he called it "an addiction second in intensity only to his nicotine addiction."[9] In the last year of his life, eighty-two and dying painfully of cancer, he still corresponded with Princess Marie Bonaparte, who had helped to rescue him and most of his family from the Nazis, about his beloved statuettes.

It was a well-informed addiction. Freud liked to read in the relevant literature, and followed excavations with almost envious interest, though when he told Stefan Zweig in 1931 that he had "made many sacrifices for my collection of Greek, Roman, and Egyptian antiquities and actually have read more archeology than psychology,"[10] the first half of the statement is more credible than the second. Doubtless Freud knew his ancient history and his archeology exceedingly well, but the books on his shelves—the bound volumes of journals he helped to edit, the books he read, and the books he wrote—reaffirm that the center of his attention was always the human mind, a dominant concern to which all the others, including his collecting, were tributaries. But the ancient world was a privileged tributary: some of the most prominent pictures on his walls, like that of Abu Simbel over the analytic couch, are commentaries on an inexhaustible interest. And it is certain that he made sacrifices to his addiction, especially in his earlier years, when he was an impecunious, struggling innovator in mental medicine. His letters to his family and his best friends are punctuated with reports of purchases he could not resist, bargains he could not pass by. "The ancient gods still exist," he wrote to Fliess in the summer of 1899, "for I have bought one or two lately, among them a stone Janus, who looks down on me with his two faces in very superior fashion."[11]

What, beyond the sheer pleasure in collecting, did Freud's collecting mean to him? Like other mental events, his addiction, too, was overdetermined.[12] His letters suggest that what he called his "partiality for the prehistoric"[13] had several animating causes. "I have now adorned my room with plaster casts of the Florentine statues," he wrote to Fliess in December 1896. "It was a source of extraordinary refreshment for me; I am thinking of getting rich, in order to repeat these trips. A congress on Italian soil! (Naples, Pompeii)."[14] For one thing, then, Freud's Janus heads and terracotta statuettes were simply gratifying, pleasing to the senses of sight and touch. For another, they took him out of his daily routine and, even better, the often contemptible present. When he was young and poor, Freud had felt alone and embattled; after he became something of a celebrity and, though not rich, prosperous, he retained an ironic distance from his fame and a deep skepticism about human motives in general. For a healer, it has been justly observed, Freud had a strikingly low opinion of the human animal. Much happened to him across the years, much happened that pleased him. But the unreceptive world of Vienna never changed; neither did the hatred the educated mob felt for Freud the indiscreet discoverer, nor the hatred of that larger mob, educated and uneducated, for Freud the unrepentant Jew. "Something in me rebels against the compulsion to go on earning money which is never enough," he wrote glumly to his trusted Sàndor Ferenczi in early 1922, "and to continue with the same psychological devices that for thirty years have kept me upright in the face of my contempt of people and the detestable world. Strange secret yearnings rise in me—perhaps from my ancestral heritage—for the East and the Mediterranean and for a life of quite another kind: wishes from late childhood never to be fulfilled."[15] To contemplate his antiquities was to conjure up, in cheerful moods, trips taken and trips yet to take, and, in moments of discouragement, a world he liked better than his own. Writing to Fliess from Berchtesgaden in August 1899, he announced that on the next rainy day he planned to walk to his "beloved Salzburg," where he had recently "picked up a few Egyptian antiquities. These things put me in a good mood and speak to me of distant times and lands."[16]

But Freud was a psychoanalyst first and last; he would have permitted no obsession to dominate him so completely for so many years if it had not been somehow relevant to the science that was his life. Collecting antiquities both freed him from his work and brought him back to it. It is striking, and has not gone unnoticed, that Freud liked to draw on archeology for his metaphors. In the early *Studies on Hysteria*, which he wrote with Josef Breuer, Freud employs such metaphors unmistakably and a little self-consciously: "In this, the first complete analysis of a hysteria that I undertook"—the analysis of Fräulein Elisabeth von R.—"I arrived at a procedure which I later elevated to a method and deliberately employed: the procedure of clearing away, layer by layer, the pathogenic psychical material which we liked to compare with the technique of excavating a buried city."[17] And in *Civilization and Its Discontents*, one of his last, most profound essays, Freud illustrates the "general problem of preservation in the mental sphere" by means of an analogy: the "growth of the Eternal City," which is really a series of cities, of which some of the earliest fragments survive—or, rather, have been recovered through excavations—side by side with ruins of later buildings. The human mind bears some resemblance to this evolution of many-layered Rome. But only some: Freud, having drawn the archeological analogy at length, cheerfully abandons it before the difficulties of representing historical succession by spatial pictures.[18] Freud is always willing to play with metaphors: they have their uses. But they are not proof; they are only metaphors.

Yet metaphors, as Freud would have been the first to assert, are rarely *mere* metaphors. They may be conventional locutions, the common property of many writers. And the mental image of the archeologist uncovering buried truths seems obvious enough to be consistent with the work of many psychologists. Yet employed as frequently and as pleasurably as they are in Freud, these analogies are likely to point to deeper meanings. Here, as elsewhere, dogmatism is thoroughly out of place. But there is at least some evidence that Freud envied Schliemann, who had uncovered ancient Troy layer by layer; envied him partly for his triumph, partly for his good fortune of realizing in adult life a boyish fantasy: "The man was happy as he found Priam's treasure," he told Fliess, "for happiness comes only from the fulfillment of a childhood wish"—a dictum significantly, and a little pathetically, followed by a renunciation: "That reminds me: I won't be going to Italy this year."[19] Fortunately, Freud did not need to rest content with envying Schliemann: he equalled him. At least once, Freud compared an analytical success with the discovery of Troy: buried underneath a patient's fantasies, he reported to Fliess in 1899, he found "a scene from his primal period (before twenty-two months), which satisfies all requirements and into which all remaining riddles flow; a scene that is everything at the same time, sexual, innocuous, natural, etc. I still scarcely dare really to believe it all. It is as if Schliemann had once again dug up Troy, hitherto thought legendary."[20] Let others compare him to Copernicus, to Plato, to Moses; he enjoyed, and sometimes played with, such comparisons. But he also took pleasure in the less exalted if still distinguished identification with a great explorer of the human past.

Beyond indulging such private fantasies, Freud found the comparison of psychoanalysis to archeology apt in a literal sense: to his mind, the scientific excavation of prehistoric remains described psychoanalytic procedures more accurately than any other comparable discipline. Like the archeologist, the psychoanalyst confronts promising but deceptive surfaces, which hint at, but in no way guarantee, strange discoveries. Like the archeologist, he must take care not to destroy his site with his probes; he must be patient, deft, delicate. Like the archeologist, too, he is a practical scientist guided by theoretical constructs open to revision.

All scientific disciplines are, of course, committed to the search for facts or laws not yet known, but the truths of psychoanalysis and of archeology are concealed in a particular way: to make the visible a dependable guide to the invisible requires the act of interpretation. For both sciences, the evidence is tantalizing and fragmentary, and both find it rewarding to work back from the present to the past and forward again from the past to the present: their materials appear in strata distinct from, yet historically and instructively related to, one another. And both, working as they do with fragments, make the disciplined leaps of a schooled imagination; as the archeologist reconstructs complete statues and whole temples from bits of busts and ravaged columns, so the psychoanalyst reconstructs the origins of a neurosis from distorted memories and involuntary slips. In the preface to his case history of "Dora," Freud makes this analogy explicit: "In face of the incompleteness of my analytic results," he wrote, "I have no choice but to follow the example of those explorers who are fortunate enough to bring to the light of day after long burial the priceless if mutilated remnants of antiquity. I have restored what was incomplete, following the best models known to me from other analyses; but, just like a conscientious archeologist, I have not failed to mention in each case where my reconstruction picks up and authentic parts end."[21]

Yet the neatest comparisons have their limits of application. The archeologist's material "resists" his inquiry in a metaphorical sense alone; the psychoanalyst's faces the literal unconscious resistance of his patient. I have called psychoanalysis the science of candor; it is also the science of suspicion—suspicion systematized. For just as civilization is a web of deceptions, the mental life of the individual is a highly sophisticated system of falsity: of sublimations, displacements, reaction formations. Not even dreams are safe from the sly work of the censor who lives in us all, denying the undeniable, making palatable the unpalatable—especially to ourselves. And the more wicked the secret wish, the more elaborate the screen behind which it labors for its fulfillment. Hence the psychoanalyst must be trained to distrust the most plausible explanations, reconcile the most palpable contradictions, seize the most evasive hints, and make sense of the most impenetrable nonsense. Digging down from layer to layer, he seeks the buried city. Incomplete as the archeological metaphor may be for Freud's life work, it is suggestive and elegant. What is obscure must be made clear, what is latent must be made manifest: that is probably the most important meaning that Freud's crowded shelves sustain.

Style of a Scientist

In September 1907, Sigmund Freud reported to his wife from Rome that he had just come upon "a dear familiar face" in the Vatican. "The recognition," he added, "was one-sided, for it was 'Gradiva,' high up on a wall."[22] One-sided as it was, the encounter gave Freud, as he said, great joy. This ancient bas-relief, showing a young woman stepping along gracefully, if a little emphatically, was a well-preserved and handsome object. Beyond this, it reawakened cheerful, still vivid memories: just a year before, Freud had written a psychoanalytic study of Wilhelm Jensen's novella, *Gradiva*, a story inspired, as it happened, by a cast of this very relief. He had found the subject congenial and the writing easy. In May 1907, shortly after he had published "Delusions and Dreams in Jensen's *Gradiva*," he told Jung, "It was written during sunny days, and I derived great pleasure from doing it."[23] Actually, it was Jung, a welcome recent addition to Freud's embattled clan, who had first called Jensen's novella to Freud's attention, and it was partly for Jung's sake that Freud had performed his literary psychoanalysis.

His Roman encounter, resonant with unmixed positive memories so rare for Freud, pleased him so much that he bought a cast of *Gradiva* for his consulting room and placed it at the foot of his analytic couch. As if to leave no room for doubt that this piece of art intersected, as it were, emotionally with his work, Freud hung to its left a small reproduction of Ingres's "Oedipus interrogating the Sphinx"—of all artistic subjects the most pregnant anticipation of the psychoanalyst's organized inquisitiveness. On this narrow space of wall, archeology and psychoanalysis met and merged.

They do so even more emphatically in Jensen's novella, or rather, in Freud's interpretation of it. The patient-protagonist of *Gradiva* is an archeologist, Norbert Hanold, a withdrawn, unworldly Northerner who finds clarity and cure through love in southern Italy, in sun-baked Pompeii. Hanold has managed to repress the memory of a girl with whom he had grown up and to whom he had been much attached. Visiting a collection of antiquities in Rome, he stumbles upon a bas-relief depicting a young and charming girl with a characteristic gait. He names her "Gradiva," the girl who steps along, and hangs a plaster cast in a "privileged place on the wall of his study, for the most part crowded with book cases"—just as Freud, later, was to hang his plaster cast of the same relief. Something, especially the stance of the figure, fascinates Hanold. It emerges that what makes the young woman irresistible to him is that she reminds him, though unconsciously, of the girl he had loved and "forgotten" for the sake of his profession. He has a nightmare in which he sees "Gradiva" on the day of Pompeii's destruction, and he begins to weave a network of delusions about her. He mourns her passing as though she were a beloved contemporary, not someone who had died under the lava of Vesuvius in 79 A.D. He travels to Italy under the impulsion of nameless feelings and ends up in Pompeii, driven by the same inexplicable obsession. And there he sees "Gradiva" in the street and fancies himself back in ancient Pompeii on the day of its inundation. "His science," Freud comments, "has now placed itself completely into the service of his imagination."[24] The young woman turns out to be real, and German; "Gradiva" is, of course, the girl he had once loved. She is not only lovable but clever; she recognizes Hanold's archeological delusion for what it is: there was, she tells him, "a grandiose fantasy lodged in your head" of looking upon her here, in Pompeii, as before, as "something dug up and restored to life."[25] She knows that she can be restored to real life for Hanold only if she can help him to disentangle his fantasies. At the end of her "treatment," when Hanold suddenly asks her to walk ahead of him, the girl, understanding his appeal, steps forward in the gait he had first seen on the bas-relief. She has used his delusion in the service of his recovery.

Freud, a reader of demanding tastes, acknowledged that Jensen's novella was scarcely a distinguished work of literature, but he defended its psychological perceptions: sentimental though it may sound, "one must not despise the healing potency of love against delusion."[26] And he found it notable that in making the living "Gradiva" imitate the gait of the antique relief, Jensen had offered his reader the "key to the symbolism" which Hanold had employed to disguise "his repressed memory"—namely, archeology. "There is actually no better analogy for repression, which both makes something in the mind inaccessible and preserves it, than the burial that was the fate of Pompeii and from which the city could reappear through the work of the spade."[27] Freud approved of Jensen endowing *Gradiva*, no doubt unconsciously, with such psychoanalytical techniques as the fostering of associations and the interpreting of dreams. If in one way archeology was the agent of Hanold's neurosis, it was in another way instrumental in his cure.

While Freud's "Delusions and Dreams in Jensen's *Gradiva*" throws bridges from his profession to his passion for collecting, it also links psychoanalysis to another lifelong interest, literature, to weave an intricate intellectual pattern. "Gradiva" was his first published psychoanalysis of a literary work, an inquiry into "dreams that have never been dreamt at all."[28] He had tried his hand earlier, privately, at similar analyses of short stories by Conrad Ferdinand Meyer, one of his favorite modern writers; he had found Hamlet's hesitations immensely instructive; he had drawn his master metaphor, the Oedipus complex, from Sophocles, a metaphor (or, rather, a model) more commanding than any that archeology could supply. And he sometimes said that imaginative writers, in their own intuitive way, were doing his kind of work.

The interplay among Freud's work and his interests is even more active than this. The most instructive implication of Freud's collecting antiquities was, as I have said, "What is obscure must be made clear." That prescription propels us, without strain, into the felicities of Freud's style, for leading his analysands to be clear about themselves was instrumental in making things clear to himself. And making things clear to himself was part of a wider enterprise: making things clear to his readers.

Freud the man of letters has been abundantly celebrated; the Goethe Prize was awarded to him in 1930 as writer and scientist "in equal measure."[29] Professional craftsmen like Thomas Mann or Stefan Zweig valued him not only as a savant, but as a colleague. And all of Freud's biographers devote an obligatory page or two to the efficiency and beauty of his prose. Not without reason, Freud's stylistic achievement is all the more remarkable considering the spectrum of his publications: introductory lectures to university audiences, technical communications in medical journals, ambitious speculations for a literate public. And Freud's published case histories—a genre that normally repels grace or wit—are classics in the literature of detection.

Freud was a born writer who never neglected the essentials of his craft. So far as I can determine, he had no program; he did not train himself to become a writer. He acted naturally and intuitively as a literary man from the beginning; his earliest surviving letters demonstrate that his energy, wit, and lucidity were not painfully acquired but were part of his character. In this sense, Freud was not a stylist at all; he was most forceful, most amusing, most reasonable, most persuasive when he was most himself. And he was himself—which is to say, he could draw on his deepest inner resources, blocked by a minimum of conflicts—most of the time. That, after all, was what his self-analysis was about.

However informal and unacademic his growth as a writer, it is evident that he chose the right means and the right models. He disciplined his ear by reading French and English all his life, and his pen by translating books from both languages. He read continuously and intensely, though, of necessity, not all his reading was for pleasure, or gave him pleasure. Working his way through the abundant technical literature for *The Interpretation of Dreams*, his first masterpiece, he comically complained to Fliess that this kind of reading was "a terrible punishment imposed upon all writing."[30] Freud could derive instruction even from the laborious syntax and rebarbative vocabulary of academic writers; he learned what to avoid. But his real teachers were stylists who were enemies of obscurity and strangers to jargon. While Freud explicitly acknowledges a debt only to Lessing, that spirited polemicist who created modern German practically singlehandedly, he highly valued, and must have absorbed, the qualities that distinguished Goethe and Zola, Heine and Burckhardt: vigor, precision, clarity. Late in life, Freud recalled that it was a public reading of Goethe's "beautiful" essay on Nature that set him on the road to medicine—an instructive acknowledgment in that it seems to have been not simply Goethe, the rhapsodic naturalist, who moved Freud to his choice of career, but Goethe, the beautiful stylist.[31]

Among the most dependable proofs of Freud's professionalism is the size of his output. Freud practiced in the only way a writer can practice: by writing whenever he could find, or make, the time. In the early years, when he had few patients, he spent more time in his study writing than in his consulting room analyzing. But later, when he devoted ten or more demanding hours a day, five days a week, nine months a year to his psychoanalytic practice, and was compelled to write late at night, on Sundays, or in the midst of his summer vacation, he continued to publish extensively. However sincere his professions of indifference to the world, however serious his contention that one writes principally to satisfy an inner need, however pronounced his pessimism about winning recognition for his unsettling theories, his urge to communicate those theories to others agitated him from the beginning. It remained so to the end: the last book he undertook, and did not live to finish, was a splendidly compact primer, *The Outline of Psychoanalysis*. In that fragment, as in his completed writings, his style was supremely right for his intentions.

While Freud was a natural writer, his cordial relations with literature were problematic to him. He conceded that poets and novelists were often right and profound about human motives and human conduct; they seemed to dredge up from their unconscious perceptions and insights that had often taken him, the scientist, years to discover and to demonstrate. The comparisons that the world found all too tempting to draw between the poet and the psychoanalyst were invidious: they made Freud's investigations look laborious, his discoveries imprecise and, in the derogatory sense, imaginative. When in 1896 the distinguished neurologist Krafft-Ebing dismissed Freud's theories about hysteria as "a scientific fairy tale," he chose, doubtless quite unconsciously, the very metaphor that would touch Freud at his most sensitive spot. Freud, the great man was insinuating, was guilty of perpetrating mere literature.

In the early 1890s, when he was starting his career as an innovating psychologist, Freud was still defensive about such charges. "I have not always been a psychotherapist," he wrote in his account of Fräulein Elisabeth von R., and he confessed that it still struck him as "odd that the case histories I write should read like novellas and that they lack, as it were, the serious stamp of science. I must console myself with the thought that the nature of the subject is evidently more responsible for this than my predilection." It so happens, he went on, that in hysteria traditional local diagnoses and electrical reactions lead nowhere, "while a thoroughgoing description of mental processes such as we are used to getting from imaginative writers permits me, in employing a few psychological formulas, to gather some kind of insight into the course of a hysteria."[32] Throughout his life, Freud was sensitive to being characterized as an artist; no matter how flattering the formulation, he disliked and distrusted it as just another form of resistance to the severe scientific propositions of psychoanalysis. But defensiveness was, for Freud, never enough, and he developed a position on the place of style in his discipline: he came to see psychoanalysis as a peculiar science which has, like other sciences, its appropriate mode of discourse but must, unlike other sciences, resort to literary devices which at once elucidate and endanger its theories. Since the materials of psychoanalysis are intimate, concealed, difficult to define and impossible to quantify, it needs analogies, mental pictures. They may be inexact, but they are indispensable.

Psychoanalytic rhetoric, therefore, as founded by Freud, was by its nature rich in metaphor. The persistence of repressed memories "beneath" later experiences and the efforts of the psychoanalyst to "dig" below manifest dreams called, as we have seen, for metaphors from archeology. The organization of the mind—id, ego, and superego—could be clarified with borrowings from topography. The array of resistance to wounding truths, and of adaptation to the imperatives of culture, was so diversified that it invited Freud to draw analogies from the most varied of human occupations: warfare, politics, cookery, travel, family life, the arts. What could be more graphic than Freud's picture of a censor performing the unconscious work of repression and distortion? of mental defenses against sexual impulses as dams restraining raging floods? of the psychoanalyst conjuring up, and wrestling with, vicious and savage demons?

The services that such devices could perform for psychoanalysis were not confined to the vividness they lent to presentation. At least some of the metaphors, comparisons, and analogies that Freud so vigorously employed were, in his mind, almost literally descriptive: to assimilate mental life to warfare, like assimilating psychoanalysis to archeology, said something that was true rather than just picturesque. More than that, to draw the map of human experience as crisscrossed by the roads of analogy, was to illustrate a conviction with which Freud, the nineteenth-century materialist, began his psychological inquiries, and which his accumulation of data and of theories would only strengthen: that human nature, however varied in its forms of expression, rests on essentially simple elements. Analogies disclosed substantial relationships: neurotics were like children or "savages," dreams like fantasies or psychoses, the public's resistance to psychoanalysis like the patient's resistance to his own analysis, not only apparently or suggestively but actually. Freud was aware that the scientist must not be dominated by the linguistic instruments that he himself has chosen; "psychology," he wrote in 1926, in *The Question of Lay Analysis*, "we can describe only with the aid of analogies. That is nothing unusual; the same is true elsewhere. But we must keep changing these analogies; none of them bears up long enough."[33] Whatever the limits of metaphor, Freud's ambition to discover far more than an explanation of hysteria and to solve far more than the mysteries of neuroses, to construct, in short, a psychology of general validity, was supported and exemplified by the language he used.

Metaphors and analogies were only some of the literary devices at his disposal; Freud resorted to many stratagems of persuasion. While he was, as I have said, always himself, and his writing the most direct and most expressive scientific prose we have, his artlessness was a high form of art. He was too alert to overlook himself as his greatest asset. But he was not self-conscious about his unselfconsciousness; he did not cultivate informality in the calculated manner of the English gardener planting a wilderness. "A clear and unambiguous manner of writing," he said in *The Psychopathology of Everyday Life*, "teaches us that here the author is at one with himself," while, in contrast, "where we find a strained and tortuous expression," we recognize the presence of an "inadequately settled and complicating idea or the stifled voice of the author's self-criticism."[34] It was rare for Freud, the writer, not to be at one with himself.

Awareness of self implied, for Freud, awareness of the others whom he wanted to reach, to persuade, to enlist. He wanted to make sure, he told a correspondent in 1932, not to fall into the posture of "isolated lecturing," and to keep intact the mode of discussion.[35] Awareness is, of course, the psychoanalyst's professionally cultivated characteristic. He is trained, as I have suggested, to notice what has gone unnoticed. Changing expressions, habitual gestures, unusual responses, casual slips, excessive emphases, slight hints all, provide evidence for concealed truths. And the slighter the hint, the more rewarding the work of interpretation. In fact, the psychoanalyst becomes the detective of absences: of subjects dropped, overtures rejected, silences prolonged. "He who has eyes to see and ears to hear," Freud wrote with supreme self-confidence in his account of "Dora," "grows convinced that mortals can conceal no secrets. He whose lips are silent, chatters with his fingertips; betrayal oozes through every pore."[36] Freud's case histories are instructive on this point; they are studies in the psychoanalyst's sensitivity. Examining Fräulein Elisabeth von R. in 1892, Freud noticed that when he "pinched or pressed the hyperalgesic skin and muscles of her legs, her face assumed a peculiar expression, one of pleasure rather than of pain. She cried out—I could not help thinking: as though with a voluptuous tickling—her face flushed, she threw back her head, shut her eyes, and bent her body backwards." And he significantly adds: "All of this was not very obvious but still clearly noticeable"[37]—noticeable, that is, to Freud. Again, in 1902, "Dora" came to see him, fifteen months after she had broken off her treatment, "to finish her story and once again to ask for help." Freud was not persuaded: one look at her expression was enough to "convince me that she was not serious with her request."[38] And in 1907, when Freud was listening to a patient known in the literature as the "Rat Man," he observed "a very odd composite expression" on the Rat Man's face as he recounted, with evident revulsion, some peculiarly sadistic punishments practiced in the East. Freud decided to read that expression as "one of *horror at a pleasure of his unknown to him*."[39] It was a tenuous but sufficient clue to support a grave, and, it turned out, decisive interpretation.

An observer so finely attuned to moods and meanings could scarcely help being aware of his audiences. Freud's new science was unfamiliar and in many ways repellent; it offered no comfort to the prudish and no rewards to the prurient; it consorted, in the name of science, with the grossest of superstitions: dream interpretation. Worst of all, it attacked mankind in its most vulnerable spot, its self-esteem. If Freud had not been a scientist of the utmost probity, resolutely refusing to dilute his message or to hunt for popularity, the acceptance of psychoanalysis would have come sooner. If Freud had not been, with all his probity, an advocate of genius, the acceptance of psychoanalysis would have been indefinitely delayed.

Freud's strategies of persuasion all come back to Freud presenting himself as an explorer retracing his steps for the benefit of an intelligent and sympathetic, if inadequately informed, listener. His strenuous voyage has more than repaid the strains it imposed by the unexpected and unexampled discoveries that had come along the way, and that had culminated in the historic solution of an ancient mystery, the riddle of the Sphinx. Freud acknowledged, without embarrassment at his failures or pride in his modesty, that he had taken wrong turnings at times; some seductive trails had led nowhere and some likely looking terrain had yielded only dry wells. But he wondered out loud whether such frustrating detours were not the distinctive fate of the man who is first, of the pioneer who hacks a trail through uncharted jungle so that others may walk in safety—and patronize him. He recognized that the routes his landmarks had compelled him to follow seemed devious, and that the spoils he claimed were unpalatable. He knew that his critics were calling him doctrinaire and authoritarian. He regretted the metaphors widely used to discredit him: to the best of his self-knowledge, he was neither jealous father nor manipulative politician, mad prophet nor infallible pope. He had to insist on the authenticity of his outrageous discoveries because they were, however outrageous, authentic; the court of experience, from which there is no rational appeal, continually confirmed his findings. It was true that no one had yet permitted himself more than a brief, shocked look at the fundamental realities he had been the first to lay bare; such conduct was only a vast collective piece of resistance, proof not that his disagreeable truths were false, but that they were disagreeable. After all, in suitably disguised form—in myths, fairy tales, and tragedies, in the aphorisms of moralists and the folk wisdom of nursemaids—they had sometimes risen to the surface of man's consciousness, only to be rapidly repressed once more. He could understand the resistance, and explain it, along with the facts it resisted. He could be so generous and so understanding because he was a reasonable man speaking to reasonable men; he and his audiences, after all, shared the same literary culture and held the same moral values. If he quoted Goethe to them, or Shakespeare, they would recognize the allusion; if they regretted the beastliness of humanity he had uncovered, so did he. He could see without difficulty why his listeners might hesitate and object: had he not gone their way before them, experienced the same hesitations, offered the same objections?

It was his capacity for feeling the feelings of his audience, his gift for anticipating objections and thus disarming them, that made Freud into what I have called an advocate of genius. It was his empathy raised into a principle of style that led him to take his readers and listeners into his confidence, proceeding before their eyes to develop his argument, deploy his evidence, and build the proofs on which he would rest his conclusions. It was this style of empathy that made him cast some of his writings, and not his popularizations alone, in the form of dialogues, and to give his adversaries arguments sound enough to keep the debate interesting and compel him to stretch his powers of persuasion to its limits. This, too, is why he acknowledged patches of ignorance, incomplete cures or even complete failures, and, in some matter-of-fact yet powerful postscripts, changes of mind; his science, he says over and over again, explicitly and implicitly, is after all still very young and will always be very difficult.

Freud had a picture in his consulting room, on the short wall, above a glass cabinet crowded with antiquities, that, suitably interpreted, documents his stylistic aspirations. It is a reproduction of Brouillet's painting of the great Charcot at work, *La leçon clinique du Dr. Charcot*, one of the most melodramatic renderings of an intellectual performance in the history of art. While an attendant holds a hysteric patient in the midst of a seizure, Charcot lectures to attentive listeners on her case. In the moving obituary that Freud wrote upon Charcot's death in August 1893, we see the reasons for Freud's choice, and for the attention that Charcot's public performances demanded, deserved, and received. Freud had worked with the pioneering Parisian neurologist from October 1885 to February 1886, and the exposure proved to be of critical importance in his development as a psychopathologist. Freud had come to know Charcot well. With other students, he had accompanied Charcot on his rounds in the Salpêtrière, identifying the ailments of the mental patients lodged there; an astonished Freud had played Adam to Charcot's God, receiving a splendid measure of "intellectual enjoyment" as Charcot named the diseases before him. One can read in Freud's obituary of his master his dissatisfaction with the old-fashioned theories and hidebound practices of Viennese medicine, and, quite as clearly, what kind of scientist and healer Freud hoped to make himself. This was not a passing identification; Freud would remember, and quote, Charcot all his life. Charcot, Freud wrote in 1893, was an unexcelled observer, a *"visuel"* who learned, and taught others, to override theory by experience. He took just pride in his discoveries, and "honest human pleasure in his own great successes." Like Freud he was not falsely modest, and enjoyed "talking about his beginnings and the road he had traveled." He was an indefatigable worker, a generous chief who put his discoveries at the disposal of his students, a discriminating scientist who could distinguish between solid knowledge and intelligent guesswork: "He would throw aside his authority to confess, occasionally, that one case admitted of no diagnosis, and that in another appearances had deceived him." And this candor linked Charcot's substance to his style, for, Freud goes on, "he never appeared greater to his listeners than when, with the most thoroughgoing account of his processes of thought and the greatest candor about his doubts and reservations, he strove to narrow the gulf between teacher and pupil."[40] Later, Freud would employ the same tactics for the same purposes.

Charcot's candor in his informal weekly addresses, those famous *"Leçons du mardi,"* was matched by the elegance of his formal lectures, each of them, in Freud's admiring words, "a little work of art in construction and composition." In translating two of Charcot's books, Freud was performing acts of piety and intellectual incorporation. But Freud was not born to be an epigone. Admiring Charcot, he became himself; what Charcot taught him, most of all, was that those artifices work best that are most natural—that, in short, honesty is the best strategy. He wrote his books as he practiced his psychoanalysis: responsibly. He might have had a beneficial effect on "Dora" if he had let her think that she was important to him. But he rejected this kind of operatic therapy. "I have always avoided playing a role, and contented myself with the less pretentious art of psychology."[41] The irony is transparent; he was not a humble man.

The Bourgeois as Revolutionary

While Freud's prose was superbly adapted to his purposes, his living quarters, which these photographs permit us to enter, offer a suggestive contrast to the ideas he generated there. It is as if Freud had been making explosives in a drawing room. Freud was an irreproachable bourgeois who fashioned for himself an unmistakably bourgeois environment but who, at the same time, developed theories about human nature and human conduct as subversive as any set of ideas in history. The impression of stunning audacity has necessarily faded with the acceptance of his psychology, the entrance of his vocabulary into common speech, and the insistent attempts—attempts against which Freud warned more than once—to soften their angularities. It is only after one has reconstructed the mental atmosphere and scientific pieties of the late nineteenth century that the full measure of Freud's revolution emerges. Yet he made his revolution in the most unrevolutionary of surroundings. Its banners and slogans are all invisible. What we see are photographs of friends, disciples, members of his family, and what I have called the profusion of things in his apartment, its orderly overcrowding: statues jammed together, snapshots jostling one another on precariously small surfaces, pictures half-hidden by other pictures. A photograph of Michelangelo's *Moses*, on which Freud wrote a celebrated essay, peeks out, barely recognizable, above another picture and some Oriental figurines. There seems to be no place for anything more. Indeed, the ornately framed mirror which hangs, rather surprisingly, in the window of Freud's study, was a present put there precisely because there was no room for it anywhere else. Freud's famous analytic couch is only the most conspicuous instance of this domestic self-indulgence; it is covered with a heavy rug, with plush pillows and throws, and built up in the continental manner to let the patient not so much lie down as lean back. Berggasse 19 abounds in the kind of visual and tactile excess it has become almost obligatory to call "bourgeois comfort." The epithet is facile, complacent, inexact, and misleading; it begs, as we shall see, many questions. But it says something about Freud's tastes and choices: he lived like the very kind of respectable professional man whose style of thinking he was to undermine beyond repair.

While Freud's faultless respectability has been the subject of much remark, it deserves—and, in view of these photographs, demands—yet one more exploration. Freud's longings for domesticity took the conventional form of middle-class ease and modest plenitude—of comfortableness, *Behaglichkeit*. In August 1882, writing to his fiancée during their prolonged and self-denying engagement, Freud listed the things they would need for their "little world of happiness": a pair of rooms, some tables, beds, mirrors, easy chairs, rugs, glasses and china for ordinary and for festive use, decent linens, hats with artificial flowers, big bunches of keys, and lives filled with meaningful activity, kind hospitality, and mutual love. "Shall we hang our hearts on such small things? As long as a high destiny does not knock at our peaceable door—yes, and without misgivings."[42] Freud's were the fantasies that generations of lovers have spun out together, looking in shop windows and reading the advertisements—thoroughly and unashamedly bourgeois aspirations.

Once settled, Freud did all the things the good bourgeois is supposed to do. He worked hard, worried about money, loved his wife, fathered six children, played cards, attended lodge meetings, fixed a nameplate—"Prof. Dr. Freud"—to his door, smoked cigars, and went on vacations. He was a responsible paterfamilias; though inaccessible during his extensive, absorbing working hours and often absent even during his long summer holidays, he was emotionally available to his children. His son Martin retained, all his life, the touching memory of his father resolving a humiliating impasse into which the boy had fallen. Out on a skating expedition with a brother and sister, he had been slapped by a stranger for a remark he had not made, had his season ticket confiscated by the attendant, and (most humiliating for a boy whose head was stuffed with chivalric notions about revenge) had a lawyer volunteer to take the aggressive stranger to court. When the children returned home, full of the day's dramatic events, Freud listened to them attentively and then asked Martin to tell him, in private and in detail, about the whole affair. What the father said in the interview to soothe the boy's feelings and restore his pride the son did not retain for long. "I think," he wrote gratefully many years later, "this is typical of all similar treatment when a trauma is successfully dealt with: one forgets not only the injury but also the cure."[43] Freud was a very busy man, but when he was needed, he was there. This was hardly the style of the unshackled Bohemian or of the self-absorbed genius.

Freud's attitude toward sexuality, which is, after all, the key to his science, is congruent with this portrait. "You don't suppose," the distinguished psychoanalyst Heinz Hartmann once asked rhetorically, "that Freud, the eminently respectable Austrian bourgeois, was *pleased* with his discovery of infantile sexuality?" Freud in fact presented himself in public as a reluctant Columbus, and we have no reason to question his self-appraisal. In April 1896, speaking in Vienna before the Verein für Psychiatrie und Neurologie, he insisted that in singling out "the sexual element" in the etiology of hysteria, he was following "no preconceived opinion of my own." Indeed, "the two investigators as whose disciple I began my work on hysteria, Charcot and Breuer, were far from any such presupposition; indeed they confronted it with a personal aversion which I shared at the outset." It was "only the most laborious detailed investigations" that converted Freud to his view, "and that slowly enough."[44] The discovery of infantile sexuality was far more painful for him, and delayed by far stronger resistance, than his theory about the sexual origins of hysteria. There is an eloquent, if involuntary, bit of evidence about that resistance: in *The Interpretation of Dreams*, Freud remarks in passing that "we extol the happiness of childhood, because it does not yet know sexual appetite"—this from the very investigator who made infantile sexuality the subject of scientific study, and in the very book in which he adumbrates the Oedipus Complex. It was not until the third edition, in 1911, that Freud added a cautionary footnote to this extraordinary passage, expressing reservations about childish happiness and innocence. But he never exorcised his original assertion, and there it remains, like a prehistoric monument to the tenacity of an older, less controversial attitude.

If Freud's views on sexuality were unexpectedly complex and ambiguous, his attitude toward the arts was simply and unambiguously conventional. What differentiated him from the average Viennese bourgeois was less his taste than his sincerity: while many often went to the opera to be publicly seen and privately bored, Freud rarely went to the opera, lest he be bored. One may trust him to be fully awake to these feelings and to have explored their possible origins. In his essay on the *Moses* of Michelangelo, a gratifying source for those who like to denigrate him as a typical philistine, Freud frankly conceded that he derived far more pleasure from the subject matter of the arts than from "their formal and technical properties," though he knew that artists value them precisely for these qualities. His principle enjoyment in literature and sculpture and, to a far smaller extent, painting and music, was to explore their effects on him. "Where I cannot do this, as for instance with music, I am almost incapable of enjoyment."[46] Considering Freud's comprehensive cultivation and ease of literary allusion, it seems ungracious as well as unjust to brand him a philistine. But his utilitarian appropriation of the goods that culture could provide suggests what I might call a higher philistinism, a consumption of culture less for its own sake than for the light it could shed on the scientific puzzles that interested him more than, and almost to the exclusion of, anything else. Hanns Sachs recalled that on one rare occasion when Freud was lured to the theater to see Max Reinhardt's production of *Oedipus Rex*, he greatly enjoyed the evening, but what gave him pleasure was a psychoanalytic train of thought that the tragedy had awakened rather than the performance. Freud made high culture pay.

Yet the presumed contradiction between Freud the bourgeois conformist and Freud the uncompromising scientist is almost wholly artificial. It follows from the plausible identification of the bourgeois with the conventional, which has itself become a convention. By the late 1860s and 1870s, when Freud was a young man, the term *bourgeois* had become a word of abuse among avant-garde artists, writers, and social critics. The bourgeois was, in a word, intolerable. But what made him intolerable remained a matter of dispute. Some damned him as a ruthless exploiter of his society, his workers, his family, and himself—as a materialist who, in his feverish pursuit of gain, stopped at nothing; he was a man with a hard face, a utilitarian philosophy, and an omnipotent checkbook. Others damned the bourgeois as the timid defender of the status quo, forever in search of safe investments, safe opinions, and safe emotional attachments —a man with conservative politics, comfortable slippers, and rolled-up umbrella. Ingenious theorists of the time, to be sure, found ways of reconciling these conflicting denunciations by seeing them as succeeding stages of historical development: the bourgeois, in this view, had begun as a buccaneer and ended as a *rentier*. But whether he was seen as the one or the other, or as both, the view was that the bourgeois loved money and hated art. And bold or timid, he was an incorrigible hypocrite about his cultural tastes and his sexual behavior. The modern ideal of privacy, so typically bourgeois, was little more than a convenient mask behind which he could cheat his neighbor, indulge his vulgarity, and enjoy his mistresses.

However telling these assaults on the respectable, however perceptive the critics who made them, there was far more to bourgeois nineteenth-century culture than this. The word *hypocrite* is a tendentious epithet that has obstructed an objective investigation of the inevitable gap between professions and performance. In any event, by no means all bourgeois were hypocrites and by no means all hypocrites were bourgeois. Working men, peasants, and aristocrats normally loved money and many of them did not hate art only in the sense that they were wholly untouched by it. Moreover, no single code of conduct, no single type of hero, properly defined the middle classes as a whole; the self-confident merchants of Manchester or Hamburg had a sense of themselves wholly different from their more dependent fellow bourgeois in Munich—or Vienna. It is no accident that the radical philosophies and avant-garde art which increasingly pervaded European culture from the middle of the nineteenth century onward were largely the work of bourgeois thinkers and writers: only a few of them were, like Marx and Engels, self-conscious renegades from their class. To be, as Freud was, a thoroughgoing revolutionary and a thoroughgoing bourgeois was by no means a paradox, an anomaly, or even a rarity.

One need not, then, step outside the boundaries of bourgeois culture to explain Freud. The struggle over respectability, over the place of the passions in conduct, was largely internal to the middle class. Freud's own views of the social stratum to which he belonged and in which he moved with ease clarify the nature and define the issues of this struggle. With a sensitivity hard to imagine today, nineteenth-century Europeans noted the manifestations and used the language of class. Movement within—or, for the most fortunate and unfortunate, movement between—classes was the staple of casual gossip and family politics, of plays and novels. Efforts at rising, or maneuvers calculated to enable one's children to rise, were the true business of most social strategies—of the schooling one sought, the marriage partner one found suitable, the taste one developed or demonstrated, the language one spoke or affected. The ladder of class was long and steep, and it had many rungs. There were many ways of being bourgeois, or, for that matter, anything else.

Underlying these refined distinctions, however, there were the gross divisions with which everyone worked. And each class, as Freud saw it, stood in a particular relationship to culture, principally in the way it expressed or restrained the will. In his view—hardly untypical for the late nineteenth century—the middle class stood in the middle, between the "lower orders," who could not afford and had never learned self-control, and the aristocracy, who could afford and had not unlearned self-indulgence. The great debate over culture, in which critics as diverse as Nietzsche and Ruskin, Matthew Arnold and Max Weber participated, concentrated therefore on the bourgeoisie. While most humans were thought incapable of postponing gratifications, the bourgeoisie had presumably learned to do precisely this, to harness its libido for work. Self-control had been the historic achievement and became the heavy burden of the middle class. The frequent breakdown of that control in orgies of impermissible gratifications was only natural: the "illicit" passions can command elemental energies. "Hypocrisy," —saying one thing and doing another—was, then, the tribute the bourgeois paid to his own rules, and the price of his inability to obey all of these rules all of the time. To claim a respectability one did not possess did more than help the individual to satisfy his desires in safety; it also helped to keep intact a social system that had produced immense results—results that did not benefit the bourgeoisie alone.

Freud's thought made a double contribution to the debate. It was not ambiguous, for Freud articulated its two aspects with his customary lucidity; it was not ambivalent, for Freud was, as usual, wholly conscious of where he stood. It was only incomplete and, by design, unsystematic; Freud never published a treatise on ethics and repeatedly insisted that psychoanalysis was a set of scientific propositions rather than a *Weltanschauung*. Besides, as Heinz Hartmann once put it in a splendid lecture on *Psychoanalysis and Moral Values*, "it is not always easy to discern" in Freud's work on the history of civilization—precisely the late essays which are always quoted in discussion of Freud's thoughts on culture—"what derives from analytic research and what is the result of his use of psychoanalytic knowledge in developing the main themes of his personal approach to history."[47] The two sides of Freud's work, the psychoanalytic writings and the cultural-historical speculations, were not identical; but they were consistent with, and implied one another. And, I must add, to deny that one has a *Weltanschauung* does not mean that one is, in fact, without one. Freud, in taking the part of science against authoritarianism or mysticism, at least implicitly supported some philosophies of life and opposed their opponents.

One side of Freud's thought has been emphasized at the expense of the other. Freud has often been hailed as a great liberator of men—and, despite that fatal phrase, "biology is destiny," of women, too. The accolade is fully deserved, and at least once Freud suggested that he thought so. In the summer of 1915, writing to the distinguished American neurologist James J. Putnam, he described himself as a highly moral man who accepted the moral rules of modern civilization without question—all except those governing modern sexual conduct. "Sexual morality as society, in its most extreme form, the American one, defines it, seems to be very contemptible. I stand for an incomparably freer sexual life, although," he confessed, "I myself have made very little use of such freedom: only in so far as I myself judged it to be allowable."[48] It was a part of Freud's inner freedom that he did not need to impose his private preferences on culture as a whole. Whatever his own practices, he reiterated that modern man enjoyed himself too little and punished himself too much. In a much-quoted essay of 1908 on the effects of modern sexual restraint on mental health, he insisted that the pressures of civilization had become excessive. "Experience teaches that there is for most people a limit beyond which their constitution cannot comply with the demands of culture. All those who want to be nobler than their constitution permits lapse into neurosis." And he adds, with his characteristic reasonableness, "They would have been healthier if it would have remained possible for them to be more wicked—*schlechter zu sein.*"[49] Freud's writings are pervaded with invitations to be more wicked: to accept eccentric behavior as normal, to give up punitive attitudes toward what were called the perversions—to accept, in short, one's instinctual life.

In a remarkable letter of 1935, written from Berggasse 19 to a woman, a stranger, who had confessed that her son was a homosexual, Freud chided her gently for not being able to bring herself to write the dreadful word. "May I question you why you avoid it? Homosexuality is assuredly no advantage, but it is nothing to be ashamed of, no vice, no degradation, it cannot be classified as an illness; we consider it to be a variation of the sexual function, produced by a certain arrest of sexual development." And he added, as consistent as he was being humane to the anguished mother, "Many highly respectable individuals of ancient and modern times have been homosexuals, several of the greatest men among them. (Plato, Michelangelo, Leonardo da Vinci, etc.) It is a great injustice to persecute homosexuality as a crime—and a cruelty, too."[50] When he addressed himself to more conventional sexual behavior, his liberalism was equally pronounced. At fourteen, "Dora" had responded with disgust to the sexual advances of an older man, a man she loved; Freud, in his report on the case, judged this rejection to be not praiseworthy moral conduct but a neurotic symptom: "I should certainly consider every person hysterical, in whom an occasion for sexual excitement elicits feelings preponderantly or exclusively unpleasurable."[51] Dicta such as these, delivered in Freud's most matter-of-fact voice, could only serve to enlarge the sphere of the permissible. His very theories pressed modern society to substitute clinical neutrality for high-minded condemnation. After all, if every human being is subject to the urges of infantile sexuality and the most murderous wishes against the most beloved persons, moral canons and cultural habits must be adjusted to take account of these overwhelming truths about human nature. And once again, style served substance. Freud was not Nietzsche; he was not, as Hartmann has said, " 'a transvaluer of values'—not in the sense, that is, that he wanted to impress on his fellow men a new scale of moral values."[52] But intentions and influence are two different things. Freud was no philosopher; he was just more effective than the philosophers. He was, partly without his active cooperation, a moral liberator.

But there is another side to Freud's social ideas that deserves equal prominence. Long before the trauma of World War I had assisted him in developing the postulate of the death instinct, long before he had portrayed human existence as a dramatic fight to the finish between the forces of life and the forces of death, he had been convinced that civilization must impose sacrifices of man's instinctual life by draining off energies from the libido and by restraining aggression in the service of social functioning. Although without such sacrifices civilization would be impossible, they had untoward, often tragic, consequences: unnecessary repression, excessive guilt—in short, neurosis. Freud saw no way out of this human predicament: mankind could not live without, and scarcely live with, exigent civilization. At best, the suffering could be alleviated, but to expect that it could be permanently cured was to indulge in the kind of magical wishful thinking appropriate to children, savages, and neurotics, but not worthy of grown men facing life, and death, with sober realism.

Freud presented this tragic vision of culture with his characteristic unwillingness to put pretty glosses on ugly truths; he had no wish to deceive himself and others. "I am far from offering an appraisal of human civilization," he wrote near the conclusion of *Civilization and its Discontents*. He had tried to keep free of "the enthusiastic prejudice" which claims our civilization as "the most precious thing we possess or could acquire, and that its path must necessarily lead us to heights of unimagined perfection." He thought he could "listen without indignation to the critic who, surveying cultural aspirations and the means they employ, suggests that one is bound to conclude: the whole effort is not worth the trouble." Freud could only hope that in this century, when human beings could exterminate one another to the last man, "eternal Eros" will "make an effort to overcome his equally immortal adversary in the struggle." This sentence, the last in the essay he published at the end of 1929, was cast in the mold of heroic optimism. Two years later, Freud added another concluding sentence, further qualifying this already guarded hope: "But who can foresee the success and the result?"[53] Despite all this, Freud, the man without illusions, rejected the response to culture that his pessimistic way of thinking might seem to imply. He disliked the socialist theories and socialist states of his day, not because he disapproved of their attacks on exploitation and on private property—he had, in fact, a measure of sympathy for both these attacks—but because he thought they had fallen victim to a utopian, wishful idealization of human nature. But while he had no faith in socialism, he had no use whatever for the celebration of irrational forces, or for the primitivism that would evade the dialectic of civilization by abandoning civilization altogether. He had not labored in the sickroom of the human mind to join the party of disease; he had not descended to the sewer of human nature to wallow in what he had found there. He was no devotee of the id; to him, the organizing rationalism of the ego and the nay-saying constraint of the superego were quite as natural as that blind, imperious agent of the will. Certainly, what he liked to do best—to work and to discover—required the activity, the enforced cooperation, of all three elements in the psychic mechanism. "I cannot imagine life without work as really comfortable—*recht behaglich*," he wrote to his good friend, the Swiss pastor Oskar Pfister, in 1910. "With me, fantasizing and working coincide; I find amusement in nothing else." He trembled at the thought, he added, of being disabled in advanced age, when ideas or words would no longer come. "With all the submission to fate proper to an honest man," he confessed to one very secret wish: "only no chronic infirmity, no paralysis of the capacity for work through bodily misery. Let us die in harness, as King Macbeth says."[54] The letter is as instructive as it is moving. There is that remnant, however small, of wishful thinking; there is the concentration on work as the single aim; there is the definition of pleasure that brings us back to the pictures on his walls and rugs on his floor—the desire for comfort and coziness. Freud was in this, as in so much else, like his fellow bourgeois. He was just more honest.

A Commitment to Truth

Honest is an old-fashioned—I am tempted to say a bourgeois—word. Today, philosophers, and the literary critics who borrow their terminology, are far more likely to speak of authenticity, of good faith, of demystification. But *honesty*, a word frankly laden with approving emotions and redolent with pleasing images of truth-telling merchants, children, or physicians, fits Freud better than the chic vocabulary of our time. Freud was a supremely honest man.

Yet *honesty*, being an old-fashioned word, is also nonanalytical. It describes a quality of intentions and actions without digging into its psychic roots. And the roots of Freud's honesty are thoroughly buried. There is a familiar dictum in his essay on Dostoevsky that is peculiarly relevant here. In that essay, Freud shows himself perfectly prepared to discuss Dostoevsky the moralist and the neurotic, but, faced with his literary stature (since he rated him highly, not far below Shakespeare), he feels helpless: "Before the problem of the imaginative writer—*Dichter*" he writes, and one can almost hear the sigh of resignation, "analysis must unfortunately lay down its arms."[55]

With the problem of the imaginative scientist, analysis is in a scarcely better position. It is not surprising that Freud, the ruthless inquisitor into the minds and motives of others, should have proved an irresistible target for psychoanalysis—often a kind of retributive and reductionist psychoanalysis which tries to discredit Freud's discoveries by denigrating his character. Whatever the animus of Freud's self-appointed analysts, the impulses behind Freud's imaginative, audacious exploration of man's unconscious are far from transparent. We can uncover the necessary and remain baffled by the sufficient causes of his work: it is far easier to understand the general conditions that made it possible than the specific conditions that turned his genius into an efficient instrument for research and translated the potentialities for scientific innovation into actuality.

The most conspicuous trait in Freud's character, indispensable to his capacity for generating insights and his patience in developing them into a general psychology, is his uncompromising commitment to truth. It was so powerful, he found it so natural, that he rarely troubled to justify, let alone analyze it. If it is impossible to elucidate completely, its principal strands—curiosity, singlemindedness, and intellectual courage—are manifest. Freud, above all, wanted to know. That his passion for knowledge had its origins in his infancy is beyond doubt; we may apply to him the general observation he offered in the case history of Little Hans: "thirst for knowledge and sexual curiosity seem to be inseparable."[56] Whatever its unconscious components, this desire was a prominent ingredient in that vitality that his most casual visitor could not help but notice and find attractive. In one respect, Freud was fortunate. He lived in an age when materialism was king, when researchers assumed—and in the "hard" sciences of physics or astronomy triumphantly demonstrated—that events follow strict causal laws. Freud fearlessly transferred this conviction, on which he never wavered, from the physical to the mental sphere. Now, to know was to subsume phenomena under general laws, rather than to call them names, and freud found, if I may put it this way, that there was more to know and less to judge than most thinking people had imagined. When Freud, following Charcot, removed neurotics from the dismissive category of "degenerates" to place them on a continuous spectrum, he was reclaiming regions of the mind from moralizing for the exercising of scientific curiosity.

Freud himself thought scientific inquisitiveness central to his character. In his letters of the 1880s to his fiancée, in his letters of the 1890s to Fliess, and in his autobiographical essays of the 1920s, he would return, over and over again, to his driving desire to confront, and perhaps to solve, what he liked to call the "riddles of life." Looking back in his late years, he noted that he had never particularly wanted to be a physician. "I was moved, rather, by a sort of thirst for knowledge, which was, however, directed more toward human affairs than natural objects."[57] And he reflected that "after forty-one years of medical activity," his "self-knowledge" told him that he had never "really been, properly speaking, a doctor. I became a doctor through an imposed deviation from my original intentions; and the triumph of my life lies in finding once more, after a long detour, my original direction." That direction was, he explicitly adds, an overpowering "need to understand something of the riddles of this world and perhaps to contribute something to their solution."[58] In the heady days of 1896, when he was piling discovery on discovery, he triumphantly told Fliess in several letters that he was returning, by a circuitous route, to his first ambition, to do original work in philosophy. His life, as he saw it, had described several identical, fortunate circles, moving more than once from science to healing and back to science.

The almost compulsive reiteration of the same formulations across more than half a century suggests the depth of Freud's commitment to inquiry for its own sake. But his fundamental intentions were even more overdetermined than these lapidary confessions would suggest. Freud was no indiscriminate lover of humanity, no professional philanthropist—benevolent stances which, in any event, he was inclined to depreciate as derivatives of sadism, as self-protective reaction formations. But he was more humane than he readily allowed. His case histories and his private correspondence disclose his pleasure in a patient's progress, his delicacy in managing a patient's feelings. Since transference—the analysand endowing the analyst with the lovable (and, sometimes, the hateful) traits of others—is the single most effective weapon of psychoanalytic therapy, Freud could scarcely neglect the highly charged emotional situation of the analytic relationship; and his recommendations, like his practice, generally placed the patient's benefit above the psychoanalyst's convenience. Manifestly, he found the labor of healing always hard and often exhausting; but often he found it gratifying as well. He experienced in his own practice the clash between the imperatives governing the psychoanalyst-physician and those governing the psychoanalyst-scientist: the physician serves his vocation by keeping things private, the scientist serves his by making them public. Fortunately, it was rare for the conflict between his two roles to assume dramatic form. When it did, Freud unhesitatingly chose science over healing. "Analysis," he wrote wryly, wittily to Pfister in 1910, "suffers from the cardinal vice of—virtue; it is the work of an all-too-decent human being, who thinks himself obligated to be discreet." Psychoanalytic matters become comprehensible only if they are laid out with a certain completeness, with much detail. "Hence, discretion is incompatible with the sound description of a psychoanalysis; one must turn into a wicked fellow," throw out one's ideals, "behave like an artist who buys paints with his wife's household money, or provides heat for his model with the furniture. Without such a piece of criminality there is no good work."[59] Satisfying his disciplined curiosity and providing materials for the progress of his science were privileged matters.

Freud was the first to admit that the imperiousness of his need to know made him seem single-minded, even one-sided. He humorously denied being a monomaniac, and it is true that he was neither a fanatic nor a bore. But his concentration on his work was absolute. As he told Fliess in May 1895, "A man like me cannot live without a hobby horse, without a dominating passion, without—to speak with Schiller—a tyrant, and I have found him. And in his service I now know no moderation. He is psychology."[60] Hanns Sachs, who thought he saw a "red thread" of work in all that Freud did, said, and wrote, suggests that "utter devotion to one single aim in life" is "neither rare nor in itself precious. It may vary from collector's mania to the highest aims; it may make a person hidebound and sterile or it may become the source of a permanent flow of inspiration." Freud, whose family and friends all understood and accepted his master passion, belonged to the second class. "Many minds have been narrowed down to a pinpoint by an exclusive interest, but to the chosen few it has served as a means to expand over earth and heaven. To Freud it offered a new universe and he gave his all in return."[61] This impression seems to have been quite general among those who knew him well: there was something downright impersonal about his concentration on psycho-analytic matters. His attitude recalls that of Frederick the Great, who took pride in calling himself the first servant of the state; Freud, with equal pride and less ideological distortion, could have called himself the first servant of his science: "Psychoanalysis," he wrote in 1935, in a late retrospective glance, "came to be the entire content of my life."[62] Five years earlier, he had begun his address of thanks for the Goethe Prize with a blunt declaration: "My life's work has been directed at a single aim."[63] This was the man who had told his friend Pfister many years before that he found life without work inconceivable, that to fantasize and to work were, at least for him, the same thing. This was the man who went to the theater to think about psychoanalysis—or, if this seems too harsh—who went to the theater and found himself stimulated to think about psychoanalysis.

To realize his overriding life's purpose, to occupy and map the terrain of the unconscious, the qualities of curiosity and concentration would have been, however valuable, insufficient. Freud's enterprise also demanded an uncommon supply of courage, the quality that translates honesty into action. One's first impulse—even Freud's—on sighting that terrain was to turn back. I have spoken of his unexampled audacity, his victory over inner resistances to his discoveries, his descent into the darkest reaches of human nature. I want to recall them here, for without them Freud's character, like his work, remains incomprehensible.

Facing up to things as they are characterizes Freud's life. It was not easy to be a Jew in Imperial Austria, especially a Jew with aspirations. In Vienna, anti-Semitism was more than the confused broodings of psychopaths; it pervaded and poisoned student organizations, university politics, social relationships, medical opinions. To be the destroyer of human illusions, as Freud was by intention and by results, was to make oneself into a special target of the anti-Semite. "Be assured," Freud wrote in the summer of 1908 to his brilliant disciple Karl Abraham, "if my name were Oberhuber, my innovations would have encountered far less resistance, despite everything."[64] Yet Freud persisted, both in doing psychoanalytic work and in calling himself a Jew. There is, in this loyalty, a kind of defiance. Freud was the opposite of religious; his view of religion as an illusion akin to neurosis applied to the faith of his fathers as much as any other. He granted the existence of some mysterious bonds that tied him to Judaism, and he attributed his objectivity and his willingness to be in a minority at least partly to his Jewish origins. But there was another element in this equation. "My merit in the Jewish cause," he wrote to Marie Bonaparte in 1926, after B'nai Brith had honored him on his seventieth birthday, "is confined to one single point: that I have never denied my Jewishness."[65] To deny it would have been senseless and, as he also said, undignified. The Jewish bond he felt was the recognition of a common fate in a hostile world.

Individualistic and problematic as it was, Freud's Jewishness made an intimate bond between him and Vienna. For Vienna, never in reality the city of operettas and flirtations, was, even in Freud's time, a city of ugly rehearsals; it made Freud the Jew suffer even more because he was a Jew than because he was Freud. But the core of his courage was neither sectarian nor local but intellectual. Books on Freud and books on Vienna have taken the link between the two for granted, as though nothing could be more patent than the debt that Freud owed to the city which, as I have said, he hated but could not leave. Some have argued that psychoanalysis had to emerge in Vienna because the prevalent sexual hypocrisy virtually cried out for someone to probe for the dominant, if hidden, preoccupation; others have argued, on the contrary, that psychoanalysis was inescapably Viennese because prevalent sexual candor provided the inquisitive psychologist with ample materials. Whatever the truth about Vienna's sexual attitudes, we are told that the city had an ill assorted but closely associated army of freedom fighters, of liberators who in some way must have inspired one another: Artur Schnitzler, Karl Kraus, Ludwig Wittgenstein—and Sigmund Freud.

It is certain that Freud was aware of Vienna and that, in some degree, Vienna was aware of Freud. He conducted many of his scientific skirmishes here, and analyzed a number of Viennese patients. He admired Schnitzler, was in turn derided by Kraus, and gave Wittgenstein food for tortured reflections. But it would be rash, and probably wrong, to conclude that the boldness of his fellow-residents somehow infected Freud with a boldness of his own. He lived far less in Vienna than in his own mind—with the positivist scientists of the late nineteenth century, with the triumphs of classical archeologists, with the example of Charcot, with the consolations of his correspondence, and with the infinitely instructive surprises of systematic introspection. Freud was, first and last, the scientist, bravely listening to the evidence, wherever it led.

This is not the place to examine the claims of psychoanalytic propositions to scientific status. What matters is that Freud's generalizations rested on experience with numerous patients—at first his alone, later enriched by that of his fellow analysts; and Freud steadily revised his insights as new information invalidated and compelled modifications of earlier assertions. He believed that what was most admirable in the scientific habit of mind, and was most unusual even among scientists, was the willingness to live with uncertainty. "Mediocre spirits," he once wrote to Marie Bonaparte, "demand of science a kind of certainty which it cannot give, a sort of religious satisfaction. Only the real, rare, true scientific minds can endure doubt, which is attached to all our knowledge."[66] He did not add, as he might have, that the capacity to endure this kind of doubt is the highest kind of courage.

It demanded, this courage, an unrelenting campaign against disguise and deception. In his letters to his fiancée, loving as they are, he reiterates the need for candor between them, the candor of friends. The obligatory tenderness that nineteenth-century middle-class men were supposed to pour out to their chosen women struck him as a form of condescension. "To live with one another," he told Martha Bernays in September 1882, "does not mean concealing from one another, or prettifying, everything disagreeable; helping means sharing everything that happens."[67] He applied the same high standard of frankness in matters of greater gravity. "The art of deceiving a sick man," he wrote to Fliess in February 1899, "is really quite uncalled for. What has the individual come to, how slight must be the influence of the religion of science which is supposed to have succeeded the old religion, if one no longer dares to reveal that this or that person is now to die?" And he added with a Stoic's piety, "I hope that when my time comes, I will find somebody who will treat me with more respect and tell me when I must be ready."[68] This was early in 1899, when Freud was forty-two. He kept to this exacting ideal when his time did come: writing from London in April 1939, very old and very ill, he told Marie Bonaparte that there was a concerted attempt to envelop him "in an atmosphere of optimism." He was being told that his cancer was receding, and his poor condition only temporary: "I do not believe it, and do not like to be deceived—*Ich glaube nicht daran, und mag es nicht, betrogen zu werden.*"[69] The one thing he did not want, and did not like to give, was dishonest consolation. That is why he treated religious and political dogmatism with contempt. The word is not too strong. He was quite unwilling to "stand up before my fellow-men as a prophet," he wrote on the concluding page of *Civilization and Its Discontents,* "and I bow to their reproach that I cannot offer them any consolation: for fundamentally that is what they all demand—the wildest revolutionaries no less passionately than the most virtuous pious believers."[70] On the rare occasions he felt compelled to lie in the service of medical discretion, he regretted it. Describing the case of "Katharine—" in 1895, he had reported that her hysterical symptoms originated after sexual assaults by her uncle. Many years later, in a footnote he added in 1924, he disclosed that the assailant had actually been the girl's father; and he concluded that, "A distortion like the one I introduced in this case should be altogether avoided in a case history,"[71] a candid effort to repair his earlier lack of candor. Freud's whole science was, of course, a systematic assault on the lies by which men live, and

48

which make them ill. But his urge toward honesty was something more than a professional rule; it was the principle of his existence.

The most remarkable, and scientifically the most rewarding, instance of Freud's honesty was, of course, his self-analysis. This long-drawn effort, tentatively begun perhaps as early as 1893 and never really concluded, has been well described and highly praised, but every new exposure to its inner drama must reawaken astonishment and admiration; it is a masterpiece of the scientific imagination, a masterpiece of the highest order. Freud had no precedents to follow when he undertook his self-analysis, no models to imitate. He had no one in Vienna to talk to, to test ideas with, and to gather courage from; he was, in that great center of cultivation and learning, wholly alone. He could count on only one friend and confidant, Wilhelm Fliess, whom he met on a few appointed occasions for scientific talk. Freud found these "congresses" refreshing and stimulating, but for the most part, Fliess was in Berlin, and Freud's sole resource was to write him long, immensely detailed letters, reporting his progress, his failures, his triumphs. Freud always learned much from his patients, but never more profitably than in these decisive years. He was a splendid listener, and he trained his sensitivity to the highest pitch of refinement, for he soon recognized that the hysterics who came to him for relief had, literally, much to tell him. They prepared him, at least in some degree, for what he was to find in himself; their dreams led him to his own dreams; their diversionary tactics, their fits of convenient amnesia, and their palpable misstatements alerted him to the resourcefulness of his own resistance.

But it was one thing to listen to his patients and quite another to listen to himself. This is what he implied when he thanked Fliess for "making me a present of an Other—*dass Du mir einen Anderen schenkst.*"[72] Yet Fliess, who in some respects and for some time functioned emotionally as Freud's psychoanalyst, was not an adequate substitute for the real thing, and Freud had to discover for himself even this rather mysterious role that his friend was unconsciously and intermittently playing for him.

The others being Other had two clear advantages for the tracing of subterranean connections and the imputation of concealed causes. They used overt signs—gestures as well as speech—which Freud found far easier to observe and absorb than the movements of his own mind, for which he had to rely solely on what Theodor Reik has called the inner ear. Moreover, Freud could accept the disreputable fantasies of his patients with schooled professional detachment, with the physician's knowing gravity. But his fantasies, as unpleasant, as contrary to his bourgeois self-image as any his patients brought to him, were, after all, his own. There was no one to lift the burden of guilt from him for rejoicing in his infant brother's death, for having wanted his beloved father dead so that he might have erotic access to his mother—no one but himself. "A certain personal distance between analysand and analyst," writes Max Schur in illuminating pages on Freud's self-analysis, "is an important condition for the development of a typical transference in a regular analysis. In the latter, of course, the analyst provides the interpretations, including those of all transference manifestations, and thus influences in a subtle way the course of the analysis. Most of this was different in Freud's case."[73]

The flatness of this formulation, like that of most pages on Freud's self-analysis, exhibits the inadequacy of ordinary speech confronting the magnificence of a historic act. The risks of bathos or banality are exceeded only by the risks of prosy understatement. Freud's self-analysis was heroic beyond ordinary heroism: he performed it outside any known context; he had to make his own rules; he could not guess at its ultimate significance for his theories or consequences for his sanity. He did not know what he did not know. At the same time, he found his immense daring intellectually intoxicating: his explorations, rigorously and patiently pursued, might provide a master key to the whole range of human experience—to art, politics, and religion no less than to dreams, slips, jokes, and sexual life. But if he was proved right, nearly all other psychologists were fatally wrong. Hence the perils he faced were external no less than internal; Freud was undertaking his self-analysis in years when his professional colleagues were treating him as a charlatan, a maniac, and, worst of all for him, a mystic. He was rightly reluctant to publish the truths he had discovered about his inner self—even more reluctant than he had been to discover them.

It is impossible to date with any precision the time that Freud began his momentous self-scrutiny. By 1893 or, at the latest, 1894, the pressure for generalization always active within him had brought him to the recognition that the mental activities his patients reported to him strikingly resembled his own fantasies, thoughts, and wishes. Freud more than once expressed regret that the impetus to his greatest discoveries had come from the neurotics who consulted him; by 1894, he knew that his work would draw all humans, stable and unstable, within a single circle defined by the same sets of psychological laws. In the early summer of 1894, he reported to Fliess his utter isolation in Vienna and his slow progress in his study of the neuroses. He was working on a project of general psychology, and, at the same time, on material he himself was generating. By May 25, 1895, in that important letter to Fliess in which he portrays himself as serving his tyrant, psychology, he reported ideas and procedures we are entitled to call, though Freud himself did not yet call them, self-analysis: "A satisfactory total conception of neuropsychotic disturbances is impossible if one cannot tie it to clear assumptions regarding normal mental processes. I have devoted every free minute to such work in the past few weeks, spending the night hours from eleven to two with such fantasying, translating and guessing—*Phantasieren, Übersetzen und Erraten*—and would stop only when I came upon some absurdity, or when I had truly and seriously overworked myself." As usual, analysis of self and analysis of patients reinforced one another: "Working with the neuroses in my practice gives me great pleasure. Practically everything is being confirmed daily, new things are being added, and the certainty of having the heart of the matter in my grasp does me good."[74] Then, on July 24, 1895, came the classic Irma dream which enabled him to understand what he was later to call "dream work." His materialist world view was beautifully confirmed: every scrap of manifest dream has its meaning, or set of meanings, and is related to the latent dream content that the analyst must excavate and interpret. Freud assigned the highest possible place to this dream in the making of his science; it was this very dream about which, in 1900, he wove the fantasy of the marble tablet that might single out his house one day. In August 1895, "after long mental labor—*nach langer Denkarbeit*"[75]—he confidently thought he had come to understand what he then called "pathological defense." With many setbacks, suffering many discouragements, he was making progress.

In 1896, after an agonizing terminal illness, Freud's aged father died. Freud had been prepared for that death, less than fully prepared for the emotions it was to release in him, and which his self-scrutiny permitted him to bring to the surface. Thirteen years later, in the preface to the second edition of his *Interpretation of Dreams*, he would note that his father's death had precipitated him into writing the book and inextricably entangled him in the most self-centered exploration in history: the book on dreams, he wrote, was "a piece of my self-analysis, my reaction to my father's death—that is, to the most significant event, the most decisive loss, of a man's life."[76] Dying was, as it were, the last service his father had done him; it aided Freud in understanding the operation of ambivalence.

The following year, 1897, was the year of decision. It was a time of intensified self-analysis, of ideas pouring out alternating with periods of paralysis, and of a setback that would have ended the inquiries of a lesser man. For some years, Freud had been increasingly impressed with the share of sexual conflicts in the making of the neuroses. He was not then, and never became, a pan-sexualist, and nothing irritated him more—and with justice—than to be accused of resorting to a single cause as the explanation of all human life. While he firmly held to the ubiquitousness of infantile sexuality and the importance of sexuality in all spheres of human existence, while he would later break with Jung and Adler largely on this issue, he was always ready to concede—or, rather, always insisted—that causes other than sexual ones helped to shape human motives, character, and conduct. To call Freud a reductionist is to distort his ideas and his teachings; while some of these distortions may feed on incautious, overly sweeping formulations of Freud's, the balance of his writings invalidates any such accusation. He knew, though he did not write about it at length, that life experiences give specific form to the working of elemental impulses. Even the Oedipus complex is far from uniform and depends in its working out on the impact of family constellations, of schooling, and of reading. But in the mid-1890s, when his psychoanalytic ideas were still in the formative stage, his patients were deluging him with tales of seduction in infancy, mainly by the father. These stories offered a convenient explanation for the onset of neurosis, which Freud was all the more inclined to accept as it fitted the theories he had been developing. In 1895, he and Breuer had jointly asserted that hysterics suffer mainly from reminiscences, and here were his patients, producing memories of traumatic events calculated to unsettle an unformed mind.

Common sense, analytic experience, and self-analysis conspired to make these stories ultimately incredible. His theory, remarkable alike for its range and its outrageousness, stood discredited. On September 21, 1897, Freud, just back from a summer's vacation, "refreshed, cheerful, impoverished," burst out to Fliess: "And now right off I want to confide to you the great secret that has been slowly dawning on me in the last few months. I no longer believe in my neurotica"—that is, in the seduction stories. He no longer knew, he added, where he stood.[77] One must visualize Freud's situation at this moment. He was forty years old, a psychopathologist with towering ambitions, impressive self-confidence, and small income. He had failed, sometimes barely, to secure the fame he wanted and thought he deserved. For several years he had been reconnoitering from an exposed outpost, with incredible tenacity, reaching for a general theory of mind. Now he no longer knew where he stood. He was like a brave officer venturing far into enemy territory only to sense abruptly that his troops have deserted him, and that, in any case, the war may not be worth fighting.

Freud recalled this critical moment more than once. In 1914 he thought that his erroneous seduction theory had been "almost fatal to the young science." When his theory "broke down under its own improbability" and its contradiction of ascertainable circumstances, "the first consequence was a stage of complete perplexity." The "ground of reality had been lost." At that time, he would gladly have given up the whole work; perhaps he had "persevered only because I no longer had the choice of starting on something else. At last came the reflection that, after all, one has no right to despond just because one has been deceived in one's expectations, but that one must revise those expectations"[78]—a typically Freudian appraisal of the situation: he knew that the world does not exist to gratify one's fantasies. In 1925, his memory was, if anything, more dramatic: "I was for some time completely perplexed. My confidence in my technique as in its results suffered a heavy blow." He needed to pull himself together.[79]

The letters he wrote in these decisive weeks tell a far more serene story. In the letter in which he announced the collapse of his theory, he observed that he felt neither in bad humor, nor confused, nor exhausted. And since he felt cheerful, he chose to interpret his doubts "as the result of honest and vigorous intellectual labor," and to take pride that, having got in so deep, he was still capable of criticism. Nor did he feel disgraced, but had "a sense more of victory than of defeat." Immediately criticizing his mood, in turn, he added that it was really not right. But was it wrong? If Freud had suffered a severe blow, and had to pull himself together, it took him little time to do so; if he felt ready to give up his work, he changed his mind practically over night. By October, within a few weeks of giving his doubts a free hand, he had turned the recognition of his mistaken trust in his patients into a triumphant instrument for theoretical advance: it gave him insight into the prominent place of fantasy in mental life. By October 3, he could announce that "the last four days of my self-analysis, which I consider indispensable for clearing up the whole problem, has been progressing in dreams and yielding me most valuable disclosures and clues."[80] He was dredging up erotic feelings about his mother whom, before he was two and a half, he had seen "*nudam*," using the Latin word in one of his rare accesses of gentility. By October 15, when he told Fliess that his self-analysis was the most important matter now in hand, he had grasped "the gripping power of king Oedipus."[81] Before the year was out, the structure of his theories needed only some final touches. As Freud told Fliess, in the paragraph in which he announced the universality of the Oedipus complex, the whole business was not easy. But "to be completely honest with oneself is a good exercise."[82] He had been just that, and psychoanalysis had been the result. It was on February 1, 1900, just after he had published *The Interpretation of Dreams*, that he exercised his honesty once again in that self-appraisal I quoted near the beginning of this essay, claiming only the quality of conquistador and denying for himself all the other qualities that, together, made him what he was. I said then that Freud was wrong, and it should be clear by now how wrong he was. "Conquistador, man of science, observer, experimenter, thinker." When that marble plaque is put up at Berggasse 19, that is what it should say.

CAPTIONS TO THE PHOTOGRAPHS

BY RITA RANSOHOFF

Plate 1

Berggasse 19: A Rainy Spring Day in May, 1938. "The street deserves its name, 'Hill-Street,' since a part of it was, even for the uneven ground of Vienna, exceptionally steep. As often happens in old cities, the two ends of the street belonged to different worlds. It started at the *Tändelmarkt*, Vienna's historic junk-market, and ended at the *Votivkirche*, a modern Gothic cathedral which dominated one of the most notable ornamental squares of Vienna, flanked by the University and other public buildings. No. 19 was in the comparatively level part of the street, closer to the *Tändelmarkt*, but in a quiet and respectable, if not exactly distinguished, neighbourhood."[1]

Plate 2

Berggasse 19, built in the 1870s, is an unpretentious apartment building of eclectic design: the facade of the lower part is Renaissance style, while the upper is decorated with classical revival detail. In 1938, the carved lions and heroic busts looked peaceably down on commercial shops: Siegmund Kornmehl's butcher store to the left of the entrance and the Ersten Wiener Consum-Vereines (the First Viennese Food Cooperative) to the right. The Freuds lived on the second floor (the Mezzanine). The windows facing the street were those of (l. to r.) Anna Freud's consulting room, her bedroom, the dining room, the family sitting room, and the sitting room of Minna Bernays (Professor Freud's sister-in-law).

In May, 1938, when Edmund Engelman made his pictorial record of Freud's home and offices, the Nazi flag was already flying over the building. The Nazis had invaded Austria in March.

Plate 3

Berggasse 19: The Swastika over the Door. Sigmund Freud's work had been burnt in Nazi bonfires as early as 1933, in Berlin. When the Nazis arrived in Vienna, they fully intended to "liquidate" the psychoanalytic movement. Aware of this, the Board of the Vienna Psycho-Analytic Society met two days after the Nazi invasion and decided that all its members should flee. They agreed that the new headquarters would be established wherever Freud himself found asylum. Freud commented, "After the destruction of the Temple in Jerusalem by Titus, Rabbi Jochanan ben Sakkai asked for permission to open a school at Jabneh for the study of the Torah. We are going to do the same. We are, after all, used to persecution by our history, tradition, and some of us, by personal experience. . . ."[2]

Freud and his family were under constant surveillance from the time of the German take-over on March 11 until the Freuds' departure on June 3, 1938. It was through the strenuous efforts of his colleagues, Ernest Jones, Marie Bonaparte, and Dorothy Burlingham, and the intercession of the government of the United States, that Freud was permitted to leave the country. Freud's friends were unable to secure release for four of his sisters, however, who subsequently died in the Holocaust.

Plate 4

The Entrance Hall: Looking Through to the Courtyard. In taking this photograph, Edmund Engelman retraced the steps of Freud's patients, of the colleagues who joined him here in scientific discussions, and of the psychiatrists who came to Vienna to be trained and analyzed by Freud. For forty-seven years, from 1891 to 1938, they all came to Berggasse 19.

Plate 5

The Entrance Hall: Looking Toward the Stairway. Not long after the Freud family moved to Berggasse 19, the Professor occupied three rooms on the ground floor for his office. The space had just been vacated by Viktor Adler, a former physician, who was leader of the Austrian Social Democratic Party. In 1907, Freud was able to acquire an apartment contiguous to his family quarters to which he moved his professional suite. In these rooms Freud worked for the rest of his life in Vienna.

Plate 6

The Entrance Hall: The Stairway. Daily, when he was still in good health, Freud descended these steps after the family meal at noon to take his constitutional. He often went to his publishers, to the tobacconist to select his cherished cigars, or to one of several of his favorite dealers in antiquities. When there were no errands to be done, Freud made the full circle of the Ringstrasse, walking, as was his habit, at an extraordinarily rapid pace.[3]

Sometimes, because of pressure of work, Freud was unable to take his walk until night. He was usually accompanied at these times by Frau Professor Freud, or his sister-in-law Minna Bernays, or one of his three daughters. On occasion, they would stop at a café.

Lou Andreas-Salomé has left us a record of one of these evening walks.[4] When she was visiting the Freuds in November, 1921, she noted in her journal, "Indeed, when we went out late at night for a walk . . . we talked now and then on different matters [than psychoanalytic ones] and he [Freud] frequently analysed Vienna, as it were; the streets under their wintry snow reminded him of the city's remotest past. One sensed how easily such a re-creation of the past came to him and one was reminded of the antique objects in his study and that the archeologist had created the psycho-analyst in him."[5]

Plate 7

The Landing. To a visitor standing here, Freud's office was to the right, the family apartment to the left. Except for his summer holidays, walks, Sunday visits to museums, and a Saturday night card game of Tarock, Freud confined himself quite closely to these quarters.

Plate 8

The Door to Freud's Office. Freud saw patients in consultation without appointment daily between the hours of three and four. We are told that because of life-long financial pressures, Freud limited himself to the use of the income from these consultations in the purchase of his antiquities.[6]

Plate 9

The Foyer Outside Freud's Waiting Room. The entrance to Freud's professional suite was unpretentious. The metal strips on the doors served as protection against burglars, a precaution not uncommon in Vienna of the thirties. Edmund Engelman had left his bag and camera case by the door, lower left.

Plate 10

The Waiting Room. Out of the first group of adherents to Freud's revolutionary theories, the "Psychological Wednesday Society," was formed and met weekly in this room. In 1908 the name was changed to the "Vienna Psycho-Analytical Society." It continued to meet here until 1910 when the space became too small to accommodate the members.

On the wall are portraits of three of the early directors of the *Internationaler Psychoanalytischer Verlag*, the publishing house founded in Vienna in 1919. Max Eitingon and Sandor Ferenczi (l. to r.) were pupils and life-long collaborators of Freud's. Anton von Freund was a friend and financial supporter of the Verlag until his untimely death in 1920.

The framed document attests to Freud's membership in the British Psychological Society.

Plate 11

The Consulting Room: View from the Entrance. Patients who came to see Sigmund Freud had often heard a good deal about him beforehand: about his controversial method of therapy and the storm provoked by his ideas in traditional scientific circles. Most likely they would have heard, too, about his theory of dream interpretation, of infantile sexuality, and about his alleged "nihilistic" views on organized religion. But they were always unprepared for their first glimpse of the consulting room. It was not widely known that this room was virtually a museum of antiquities that came from Egypt, Greece, Rome, and the Near and Far East. Wherever one looked there was rich, tactile evidence of Freud's ideas. The room immediately evoked a sense of the ages. The silent yet somehow eloquent figures of the past confronted the patient who came here to rediscover his own origins and buried history.

Plate 12

The Couch: Close-up. The couch is piled high with pillows so that the patient would be in a near-sitting position, but eminently comfortable. In fact, comfort and well-being are the keynote motifs of the room: a fire burns brightly in the tile stove at the foot of the couch. Tubes that were regularly refilled with water are attached to each side of the stove to humidify the room. The patient could cover himself with the shawl at the foot of the couch to protect against a possible draft. Freud would sit just behind the couch in an easy chair with a footstool. The room is cluttered, in late Victorian style, but in an organized, controlled, "interesting" manner. The antiquities have their place; they do not take over. The wall covering is plain, almost dark; pattern and color come from the Oriental rugs on the floor, the couch, and its adjacent wall.

Freud chose a picture of the vast Egyptian cliff temple of Ramses II at Abu Simbel to hang above the couch. Ramses II was the great imperial pharoah who fought his way from southern Palestine to Syria in the thirteenth century B.C. The temple's presence here proclaims Freud's preoccupation with the ancient past.

At the foot of the Couch. A plaster cast of the *Gradiva*, "the girl who steps along," hangs on the wall, adorned with a dryed papyrus plant. This is a copy of a Greek or Roman bas-relief. The girl on the relief was the inspiration for a book by a popular novelist, Wilhelm Jensen, a contemporary of Freud's. The book, in turn, stimulated Freud to write a paper which he called "Delusions and Dreams in Jensen's *Gradiva*," a pioneering essay in the psychoanalysis of literature. Jensen's novel, even with its cumbersome plot, was made to order for Freud. The hero, Norbert Hanold, is an archeologist, a man who has "buried" a part of his own past, his youthful love for a girl named Zöe, or "life." She disappeared, "died" in Hanold's unconscious, only to reappear in the figure of "Gradiva" on the marble bas-relief, to which he is mysteriously drawn. Zöe then actually does reappear to Hanold, in a dreamlike sequence, when he is visiting Pompeii—she is a forgotten figure come to life.

One of Freud's biographers, Max Schur, commented on the Gradiva paper, "In this work, . . . Freud permitted himself to deal with the problem of death and immortality in a manner more poetic than scientific. Immortality was seen in the continuity of 'Zöe,' life arising out of the ashes [of Pompeii]. . . . The victory of life and love over the forces of destruction and madness runs throughout Freud's work."[7]

To the left of the bas-relief of *Gradiva* is a photograph of Ernst von Fleischl-Marxow (1846–1891), a colleague of Freud's when he worked as a young man in Ernst Brücke's physiological laboratory. Freud greatly admired and respected Dr. Fleischl; he was a man, Freud said, whom he was happy to take for a model.

Below the photograph of Fleischl is a reproduction of Ingres's painting of Oedipus interrogating the Sphinx.[8] In this setting, it is a graphic reminder of Freud's discovery of the sexual wishes and fantasies of childhood, the Oedipus complex, Freud's own solution to the riddle of the Sphinx.

Ernest Jones records that on Freud's fiftieth

birthday, the small group of his followers in Vienna gave him a medallion with his profile on one side and a Greek design of Oedipus answering the Sphinx on the other. Around it was the line from Sophocles's *Oedipus Tyrannus:* "Who divined the famed riddle and was a man most mighty." When he was presented with this medallion, Freud turned pale. He explained that as a student in the University, he would stroll around the court looking at the busts of former illustrious professors. He had a fantasy that one day his bust would be there, and on it would be inscribed this line of Sophocles. In 1955, years after this daydream, Jones presented a bust of Freud to the University of Vienna to be placed in the arcade. On it was inscribed the line from Sophocles.[9]

Plate 13

Freud's Corner: His Chair and Footstool Behind the Couch. Freud placed himself in this position, of course, for technical reasons, so that his presence would not interfere with the patient's free associations. It is difficult for us to put ourselves backward in time to the moment when Freud was struggling to find techniques that would lead the way to understanding the meaning of man's psychic life. The use of the couch for free association, the "telling" of thoughts and ideas as they came into the mind; the discovery of meaning in the dream; the phenomenon of transference of feelings from significant persons in the patient's past onto the person of the analyst—all these proved to be the technical tools that led to an understanding of unconscious conflicts and symptom formation.

Freud was not the silent, uncommunicative analyst portrayed in caricature. He could be enthusiastic in his responses to his patients. On occasion he would even announce a "celebration" by getting up from his seat to select and light one of his favorite, forbidden cigars.

Plate 14

Freud's Corner: Detail. Here, above the chair where Freud sat listening to his patients, are two large framed fragments of Pompeiian-style wall paintings dominated by mythological figures: a centaur (half man-half horse) and Pan (half man-half goat). They represent aspects that are primitive, phallic, and pleasure-seeking in human nature. Below these large framed fragments, on a pedestal, sits a dignified Roman portrait head (efforts to identify it have been unsuccessful to date). It is "the Roman citizen," symbol of a nation dedicated to the rule of law.

Freud was greatly stimulated by the ancient civilizations of the Italian Peninsula. He made seven vacation trips to Italy, where he delighted in the antiquities of Etruscan towns, of Magna Graecia in southern Italy and Sicily, and of the Roman ruins throughout Italy and, especially, in Rome itself.

Here in Freud's corner the mythological figures from Pompeii and the head of the Roman citizen illuminate contrasting aspects of man: his impulsive animal nature and the civilizing influence of conscience and law. Here is a suggestion of images of the id and the superego, two aspects of Freud's hypothesis of the structure of the mind.

From left to right, below the centaur fragment,

are four drawings (only three are visible in the photograph) by Wilhelm Busch in a single frame. They are (clockwise from the top): a donkey watching an artist painting, a chick hatching out of an egg (dated January 1, 1894), a rhinoceros confronting an African native, and a fish spitting at a fly. Busch's brand of humor was extremely popular with German children growing up in the 1860s and 1870s. Freud was no exception.[10]

On either side of the Roman head are Pompeiian-style painted fragments: a sphinx, a winged goddess with a long-legged bird, a fragment with a leaf design, a silenus (a woodland deity with a horse's ears and tail), and two fragments below, an attacking lion and a swan.

On the lower left are two Egyptian fragments, the larger a papyrus in which, among others, the figures of Horus, Anubis, and Osiris, Egyptian gods of the underworld, can be discerned.

the illustrations to Philippson's Bible. I fancy they must have been gods with falcons' heads from an ancient Egyptian funerary relief."[12]

The Philippson Bible, with text in Hebrew and German, had been read with deep interest and fascination by Freud as a young boy.[13] (A complete edition, eight volumes, was in his library.) It was profusely illustrated with pictures of the Egyptian gods. Among them, the falcon-headed Horus appears a number of times.

In his self-analysis, Freud traced the anxiety in the dream "to an obscure and evidently sexual craving that had found appropriate expression in the visual content of the dream."[14] In his consulting room, almost seventy-five years later, Horus was still standing before him. (For additional material on the influence of the Horus myth upon Freud's thinking, see the caption to Plate 35.)

Plate 15

The Antiquities in Freud's View. "The immortality of our emotions . . ."[11] On the left-hand corner of the table (just in front of the shelves in the picture) stands Horus (detail below large photograph), son of Isis and Osiris, one of the most significant falcon-headed gods of the Egyptians. At the age of seven or eight, Freud had an anxiety dream which he analyzed some thirty years later. "In it," he wrote "I saw *my beloved mother, with a peculiarly peaceful, sleeping expression on her features, being carried into the room by two (or three) people, with birds' beaks and laid upon the bed.* I awoke in tears and screaming and interrupted my parents' sleep. The strangely draped and unnaturally tall figures with birds' beaks were derived from

Plate 16

Another View of the Antiquities: Directly in front of Freud's Chair. Egyptian wooden funerary figures of various periods stand on the table. Six are in human form. Horus is partly hidden behind the male figure in the front row, left. The Egyptians had several deities with the head of a lioness, but it is probably Sakmet, the fierce goddess of the Memphis cosmology, symbolizing the scorching power of the sun, who stands second from the right in the back row.

On the shelves behind is a miscellany of statuettes and vases: a large Chinese camel from the Tang Dynasty (618–907 A.D.) is easy to identify. Two shelves above it, on the left, are a classical Greek head in terra cotta (fifth to fourth century B.C.) and several Far Eastern Buddhas. On the second shelf, to the right of the flowers, is an

Egyptian cobra (Uraeus) of wood or metal, emblem of the pharoah's power, from a mummy's crown or from a piece of furniture.

afterlife: namely (l. to r.) Nephthys, Isis, Anubis, Horus, and Osiris.

Plate 17

View of the Table and Its Bookshelves. In Freud's case histories we come upon evidence of how he used his antiquities to instruct his patients on the workings of the mind: "I then made some short observations upon *the psychological difference between the conscious and the unconscious*, and upon the fact that everything conscious was subject to a process of wearing-away, while what was unconscious was relatively unchangeable; and I illustrated my remarks by pointing to the antique objects standing about in my room. They were, in fact, I said, only objects found in a tomb, and their burial had been their preservation: the destruction of Pompeii was only beginning now that it had been dug up."[15]

Centered above the bookcase is a marble bas-relief (Greek? Roman? a lid of a sarcophagus?), which shows evidence of once being broken into two parts. According to Anna Freud, her father believed it to be a scene of the "Death of Patroclus" in the Trojan War. She relates that originally only half of the bas-relief was in Freud's collection. One day an antiquities dealer appeared at the door with a piece he wished to sell to Professor Freud. It was the other half of the fragment. Freud promptly purchased it and had the two parts rejoined.[16]

Of the two Egyptian funerary stelae flanking the bas-relief, only the one on the right, illuminated by the lamp, has been described. Its inscription is to the dead Hordiefnakht as he appears before the gods who will judge his fitness for the

Plate 18

Detail of the Bookcase. The Egyptian warrior goddess, Neith, stands on the left. Freud acquired a number of figures of Neith, attesting to his special interest in her. Freud related her to his theory of infantile sexuality: in the paper "Leonardo da Vinci and a Memory of His Childhood" Freud discussed the fact that Neith, as well as a number of other Egyptian and Greek deities, were *originally* conceived of as androgynous. He puzzled over the question why the human imagination should endow the female body with a penis. From interpreting the fantasies of his patients, Freud found an answer—in the castration fears of the young boy.[17]

Plate 19

The Entrance to the Consulting Room. Engelman's sweep around the room has returned us to the entrance door. Behind us, and to the right, is Freud's chair and the couch. A small and inconspicuous door, covered in the same dark material as the walls, can be seen next to the entrance. Patients who wished to ensure their personal privacy could leave by this door without returning to the waiting room.

This door also led to Freud's examining room where his doctor, Max Schur, came daily to examine and treat him for cancer of the palate. This illness first appeared in 1923; subsequently, Freud underwent some thirty surgical procedures and was required to wear a prosthesis in the roof of his mouth which was painful and cumbersome, and made speaking difficult.

The Treatment Room. A view of the small room off the consulting room where Freud received medical treatment for his cancer.

Plate 20

The Consulting Room: To the Right of the Entrance. The single window in the consulting room lets in the sunshine from the courtyard. Over the cabinet between the window and the door hangs the engraving: *La Leçon clinique du Dr. Charcot.*[18] A hysterical female patient is being shown to members of the staff of the Salpêtrière hospital in Paris. (Freud, of course, was a student at this renowned neurological center from October, 1885 to February, 1886.) Mathilde, Freud's eldest daughter, was fascinated by this picture as a child and repeatedly asked her father what was wrong with the woman. "Too tightly laced," was Freud's reply.[19]

Plate 21

The Cabinet Between the Window and the Entrance Door: Close-up of Egyptian Funerary Objects. Atop the cabinet sit a number of carved and painted wooden figures that were placed in tombs to meet the needs of the dead. Freud was fascinated by Egyptian burial customs and the theme of death and rebirth in the afterworld. On the left are two women servants bearing provisions. Next to them are a group of men planting (Middle Kingdom, c. 2050–1786 B.C.). A large

painted figure of Osiris looms above the figures (Late Period, c. 1085–332 B.C.). Six Ushabtis, standing figures, can also be identified (New Kingdom, c. 1567–1085 B.C. and Late Period). They were named the "answerers" because it was their duty to respond to the call of their master and perform any service he might require.

Plate 22

The Cabinet to the Left of the Entrance to the Study. According to Anna Freud, a catalogue of Freud's antiquities has never been compiled.[20] We are told, however, that in August, 1914, when the outbreak of World War I made it impossible for Freud to take his usual summer holiday, he spent the time cataloguing his collection.[21] Freud began collecting on a modest scale—there is mention of the acquisition of a few pieces in letters to Wilhelm Fliess as early as 1899—and he maintained his interest throughout his life. Freud's catalogue of the collection, as it existed in 1914, however, has not survived.[22]

In this photograph we can identify the Chinese figures that stand on top of the cabinet. On the left is the figure of a lady (Tang Dynasty, 618–907 A.D.), then there is a Horse (Tang or Wei Period, 368–534 A.D.), and on the right is a smaller female figure (similar in style to the Tang Period).

A variety of Hellenistic objects are inside the cabinet. Prominent among them (second shelf, left) is a vessel in the shape of a head (Attic[?], c. 520 B.C.). In the center of this shelf is a covered bowl: a red-figured pyxis (Attic, c. mid-fifth century B.C.). There are also several figurines of the Tenagra type (third century B.C.). On the bottom shelf are three larger Hellenistic figurines (probably third to second century B.C.).

With careful scrutiny, two Near Eastern mother goddesses (from the area around modern Syria, second millennium B.C.) can be discovered in this cabinet. If you follow the rear legs of the Chinese horse standing on the cabinet down to the top shelf, you can observe the first of these. During the process of authenticating these pieces, the mother goddess (third from the right on the second shelf behind the Tenagra lady with a hat) was found to be "extremely doubtful."[23]

Freud was especially concerned about the authenticity of the pieces he selected—he carefully studied such things as the patina and areas of repair or reconstruction. When he had questions about authenticating a purchase, he would send it to the Kunsthistorisches Museum in Vienna to be validated. But in spite of Freud's scrupulous concern, his collection contains its share of inevitable forgeries.

Plate 23

The Doorway Leading into the Study. We have come full circle around the consulting room, and are facing the entrance to Freud's library and study. Among the objects visible here, directly to the lower right of the door frame, is an Egyptian sunken relief of a man with hands raised in a gesture of adoration (probably from a tomb of the early Nineteenth Dynasty, c. 1300 B.C.). Above it is mounted a Sicilian head, a votive protome (terra cotta, first half of the fifth century B.C.). Centered atop the right cabinet is a Chinese flying horse and rider (clay, from the Han Dynasty, 202 B.C.–220 A.D., or the Tang Period, 618–907 A.D.). Just behind these Chinese figures hangs an unsigned engraving of the Roman Forum. During his seven trips to Rome, Freud especially loved to wander in the Forum and on the Palatine Hill nearby.

Plate 24

Freud's Study. It was here that Freud saw prospective patients in consultation. It was here, too, that he engaged in intellectual discussion with the men and women who came to see him: Carl Jung, Thomas Mann, and Edmund Löwy (a friend from student days and a professor of archeology in Rome, who annually visited Vienna to see his family and friends). Freud's talks with visiting colleagues, Hanns Sachs, Ernest Jones, Sándor Ferenczi, Karl Abraham, Lou Andreas-Salomé, to name but a few, lasted long into the night.

The room was completely lined with books and lit by windows looking out into the courtyard. It was a quiet room. And it was here that Freud did his scientific writing.

A large statue of the Egyptian goddess Neith stands on the left side of the desk; on a pedestal in the rear corner, to the right, is an Attic black-figured amphora with a mythological scene (520–510 B.C.). As early as 1885, fifteen years before the publication of *The Interpretation of Dreams*, when Freud visited the Louvre for the first time, he wrote, "There were Assyrian Kings—tall as trees and holding lions for lap dogs in their arms, winged human animals with beautifully dressed hair, cuneiform inscriptions *as clear as if they had been done yesterday*, and then Egyptian reliefs decorated in fiery colors, veritable colossi of kings, real sphinxes, *a dream-like world. . . .*"[24] These dreamlike qualities of the anthropomorphic gods—condensed and timeless symbols—appear in Freud's discoveries about the nature of the unconscious.

Plate 25

Freud's Desk. Wreathed in tobacco smoke, Freud would write long hours into the morning. On his desk the day this picture was taken was a manuscript now believed to be his *Moses and Monotheism*. The ancient figures, in ceremonial poses, stood directly before him as he worked.

Among the objects we can identify are (back row, l. to r.): Tall figure (Roman Imperial or Greek Terra Cotta, c. 430 B.C.); Chinese Tomb Figurine (clay, Northern Wei, c. sixth century A.D.); the god Osiris (bronze, Egyptian); a carved and framed Eastern figure, Amun-Re (Egyptian); Arhat or Lohan (Far Eastern laughing monk, period unknown); Osiris; a Chinese Tomb figure depicting a foreigner from central Asia (clay, Tang Dynasty, 618–907 A.D.); Isis nursing Horus or a king; Etruscan Warrior; large head of Osiris; and, to the right of the small bronze on a pedestal, a Roman Janus head depicting Silenus and Minerva, with only Minerva visible. Front row, l. to r.: Aphrodite (bronze, Roman Imperial Times); in front of her and to the right, Falcon-head ("Kebehseneueuf," Egyptian, a lid from a Canopic jar); just above it, Near Eastern (?) figure on pedestal; to the right, mummiform figure of Ptah, creator-god of Memphis (Egyptian); small Roman Imperial bronze (Mercury [?]); another small Roman bronze (Jupiter [?]). Continuing, we see a small Egyptian bronze figure of a king with part of his right hand missing; Bastet (Egyptian cat-headed goddess); Nefertum, the son of Ptah with his lotus headdress; Neith wearing her pointed crown; and Horus as a child.

Skipping the next Egyptian figure, we come to a winged goddess (Isis?); Herishef [?]; and Sakmet, the Egyptian lioness-headed goddess, the wife of Ptah.

One Egyptian head from the statue of a private person is being used as a paper weight.

Plate 26

The Table to the Right of the Desk. We are told that Freud greeted this Chinese scholar each day when he came into his study.[25] To the left is the Egyptian figure of Imhotep holding a papyrus scroll upon his lap. In the Late Period (1085–332 B.C.) he was venerated as a god of learning and medicine: the sick and the crippled from all over Egypt flocked to his chapel at Saqqara. The Greeks identified him with Asclepius, their god of medicine. A Chinese wise man and an ancient Egyptian healer . . . reassuring guides for Freud's journeys into the underworld.

We do not know why Freud chose the figure of the minor Egyptian deity (on the right) for this special place next to his desk. The carved receptacle is filled with a miscellany of personal articles. There is also the ubiquitous ash tray. It is interesting to note the presence of an English dictionary.

Plate 27

The Greek Urn. Behind Freud's desk, this spring day in 1938, was a large Greek urn filled with budding branches. This urn is now in Golder's Green Cemetery in London and holds the ashes of Sigmund and Martha Freud.[26] (There are two

other views of the urn in the photograph above.)

The urn is a south Italian Bell Krater (late fifth or early fourth century B.C.), a gift to Freud from his colleague, Princess Marie Bonaparte. It was probably executed by a Greek artist living in Italy. Painted on one side are Dionysos seated, holding Thyrsos and Kantharos, with a standing woman (Ariadne?) holding a dish of offerings (?) and a mirror. Between them is a pillar. On the obverse side are two draped youths in conversation, one holding a walking stick, the other a tied wreath; between them is a pillar. The subjects of the two sides are very likely unrelated.

Vases of this type served as mixing vessels for wine and water at symposia. They were placed directly in a grave for a burial gift as well. It is possible that this is the second time the vase in the photograph has been used for funerary purposes.[27]

Plate 28

The Desk Chair. When sitting at his desk reading, Freud had the habit of putting one leg over the arm of the chair and holding his book in an awkward position. This chair was made especially for Freud around 1930 by Felix Augenfeld, an architect and friend of the family.[28]

Plate 29

The Study: Freud's Library. Freud was a book lover all of his life: he bought books, not to acquire rare editions or fine bindings, but to satisfy his wide-ranging intellectual interests. One-third of the books are in foreign languages: English, French, Spanish, and Italian. They are about equally divided between the humanities and sciences, not only because he was equally at home in both worlds, as some writers have commented, but because it was from the humanities that he found verification for his scientific discoveries—from myths and fairy tales, the Greek playwrights, Goethe, Shakespeare, etc.[29] The library is replete with books on anthropology, religion, history, ancient civilizations, and archeology. (There are even several volumes devoted to the understanding of Egyptian hieroglyphics and cuneiform inscriptions.)

Plate 30

The Cabinet Behind the Chair. On the top are a Chinese Tang camel and horse; between them is a Greek vessel in the shape of a sphinx. Inside the cabinet, amid the Roman oil lamps and the Eastern carved jade and ivory, there are again Egyptian statuettes: Anubis, the jackal-headed god, and Sakmet, the goddess with the head of a lioness, among others. Freud's delight in collecting Egyptian antiquities reveals itself in a charming fantasy. When his colleague Sándor Ferenczi purchased a home in Buda, Hungary, in 1930, Freud wrote him hoping he would do some excavating in his garden and thereby discover he was living on the site of a Roman villa. Freud hoped, further, that the Roman owner would have traveled in Egypt and brought back many souvenirs.[30]

Hanging on the bookcase to the left of the cabinet is a moving personal note among these impressive surroundings: a photograph of Anna Freud's dog "Wolf." Miss Freud recalls that on each birthday, Freud would be presented with a celebratory poem from "Wolf," which she had written in honor of the occasion.[31]

Plates 31 and 32

Close-up View of Corner of Study. Freud had no more space for his collection of antiquities. In this corner of the room they have spilled over onto the floor.

Plate 33

Close-up: Left Side of Study. In front of the books are photographs of several women—admired friends, two of whom were colleagues. They are (l. to r.) Marie Bonaparte, Lou Andreas-Salomé, a second photograph of Marie Bonaparte, and a portrait of the popular Parisian singer and actress, Yvette Guilbert, immortalized by Toulouse-Lautrec. Two books by her, including her memoirs, were here in Freud's library. Freud regularly attended her concerts when she was in Vienna. Freud sustained a close friendship and a lengthy correspondence with Lou Andreas-Salomé. She and Marie Bonaparte were among the first of the long line of women psychoanalysts. Marie Bonaparte published a classic psychoanalytic study of Edgar Allan Poe, and a number of articles on the psychology of women. It was to her that Freud said: "The great question that has never been answered and which I have not yet been able to answer, despite my thirty years of research into the feminine soul, is 'What does a woman want?'"[32]

Plate 34

Detail of Plate 33. The largest head, rear left, is the top half of a mummy cover (Egyptian, Twelfth Dynasty, c. 1991–1786 B.C.). This piece was sold to Professor Freud by Robert Lustig, one of Freud's antiquities dealers in Vienna from 1927 to 1938. Freud instructed Lustig to come to his house twice a month to show him pieces he had acquired. Freud was eager to own the mummy case, but felt he could not afford it. He offered Mr. Lustig a sum of money plus the choice of some objects from his collection. He opened a drawer filled with Etruscan mirrors. Mr. Lustig was so overwhelmed by their numbers he could not even stop to examine them, he said, but "took the top layer" and departed.[33]

The tip of Michelangelo's *Moses*, an enduring favorite of Freud's, is barely visible behind an unframed landscape. Among the other objects are (back row, l. to r., starting next to the large mummy cover): a Chinese Bodhisattava (Sung Dynasty, c. 960–1125 A.D.); below the framed picture of Lou Andreas-Salomé, the head of a Bodhisattava (Chinese, sixth century A.D. [?]). In the second row: Cypriote head [?] (Classical period); figure of a Monk (Chinese [?]); head of an Egyptian official (granite, Nineteenth or Twentieth Dynasty); an Egyptian block statue; a head of a Buddha (white marble, Chinese, based on a Tang Model, c. 618–907 A.D.); a bust of Seraphis (Roman, after a cult statue by Bryaxis, Original, c. 300 B.C.); a torso of Aphrodite (possibly a replica from the Roman Imperial Era of a Greek statue, fifth century B.C.).

Plate 35

The View from Freud's Desk into the Consulting Room. Freud and the patients he saw in consultation spoke across the small table beside the desk. When Freud returned to his writing after their departure, the gods were there, not unlike his patients, waiting to be understood.

Among the figures are representations of the Egyptian gods Osiris, Isis, his wife, nursing their son Horus, and a statuette of Horus as a child. The myths attached to these preeminent Egyptian gods bring together ideas that were to dominate Freud's thought. Osiris, god of the dead and of resurrection, represents the universal wish for rebirth. He was killed and dismembered by his evil brother, Seth, but his body was returned to life by Isis. The son, Horus, was born magically, like all heroes. As in the *Hamlet* theme that so fascinated Freud, Horus, the falcon-headed god of Freud's childhood dream, avenged his father's death. There are many complicated variants of the Horus-Seth struggle. In one, a castration theme appears: Seth snatched away one of the eyes of Horus and dashed it to pieces. It was restored by the god Thoth. The eye of Horus, *udjat,* "that which is sound," became a powerful amulet and assured good health.[34]

Plate 36

Freud at Work in His Study. Freud was working on the final section of the monograph *Moses and Monotheism* at the time that Engelman came to photograph the apartment. Efforts had been made on the part of Freud's family to avoid disturbing his routine. But on this particular morning, Freud had changed his schedule and Engelman unex-pectedly found him here. (See Edmund Engelman's memoir, pp. 131ff).

Plate 37

Portrait. Freud consented to sit for Engelman on the day he was discovered in the study. He was, at this period, waiting for his exit visa. He wrote his son Ernst, who had preceded him to London, on May 12, 1938, "I am sitting inactive and helpless while Anna runs here and there, coping with all the authorities, attending to all the business details. . . . Two prospects keep me going in these grim times: to rejoin you all and to die in freedom. I sometimes compare myself with the old Jacob, who, when a very old man, was taken by his children to Egypt. . . . Let us hope that it won't be followed by an exodus from Egypt. It is high time that Ahasuerus [the wandering Jew] came to rest somewhere."[35]

Plate 38

Portrait: Martha Bernays Freud (July 26, 1861–November 2, 1951). Visitors to the Freud household throughout the many years the family lived at Berggasse 19 always responded in the same way to Martha Freud. She was described as a small, lithe, and mobile woman, somewhat reserved in social relationships, but unerringly kind and humane in her outlook. She bore her six children in ten years; her life was deeply committed to the responsibilities placed on her by her family. Despite the very "modern" personal style of the numerous brilliant women who were involved in the early psychoanalytic movement, Martha Freud chose the traditional and highly respected role of wife of a professional man, and mother of a large family. She apparently knew what was required to meet the needs of a man as complex and creative as her husband. Nevertheless, her taste clearly dominated the family apartments and, probably, the tone of family life.

Plate 39

Portrait: Anna Freud at the age of forty-two. Anna was a practicing psychoanalyst by this time. She had already written her seminal book, *The Ego and the Mechanisms of Defense* (1936). On March 22, 1938, not long before Edmund Engelman took these photographs, the Freud apartment at Berggasse 19 had been invaded a second time by S.S. men. Anna Freud had been arrested and taken to Gestapo headquarters. It was only by the use of her wits and great personal courage that she succeeded in being released.[36] This extraordinary portrait suggests Miss Freud's deep concern in her struggle to free her father and family from the Nazis.

Plate 40

Anna Freud's Consulting Room. An etching of Professor Freud by Ferdinand Schmutzer, c. 1920, hangs over the couch. Of Freud's six children, Anna was the only one to enter the field of psychiatry. Her father came to depend upon her as his illness began to limit his mobility. In effect, Anna Freud served as her father's executive secretary in the scientific business of the Vienna Psychoanalytic Society and the International Psychoanalytic Association. She often at-

tended meetings or public events on his behalf. In August, 1930, she read an address by her father in Frankfurt, after he had received the Goethe Prize for Literature.

Plate 41

Anna Freud's Consulting Room: Second View. Here, in Anna Freud's consulting room as it appeared in 1938, there is a modern bookcase, designed at her request by the architect Felix Augenfeld. To the right of the tile stove is a "folk art" hand-crafted chest.

Freud and his entire family cherished their privacy. We are afforded an occasional glimpse into their lives in the letters and diaries of friends. Lou Andreas-Salomé wrote in her journal of her stay with the Freuds in November 1921. Every morning, she noted, was spent in Anna Freud's room where the two women engaged in theoretical discussions; Lou Andreas-Salomé would always be wrapped in an afghan and Anna Freud would be sitting near the stove for warmth. Freud joined in their talks between each of his analytic hours, and Lou Andreas-Salomé comments on the evenness of his mood, his serenity, and his kindness.[37]

Plate 42

The Family Quarters: Aunt Minna's Sitting Room. There is no reason to believe that Freud was not completely at home in the family apartment that was so unprepossessing in its furnishings and so much in contrast to the atmosphere of his study and consulting room. (See Peter Gay's essay, pp. 33–34.) On top of the bookcase is a small reproduction that appears to be the famous "Boy with the Thorn." (The original is in the Capitoline Museum in Rome.) It speaks to the contrast between the objects of Freud's sanctum and that of the family quarters.

Minna Bernays (1865–1941) joined the Freud household in 1896. She had been engaged to Freud's friend, Ignaz Schönberg, who died of pulmonary tuberculosis some ten years earlier. "Tante" Minna remained with the Freuds the rest of her life. She was an extremely bright, outspoken, and literary woman, given to epigrammatic sayings. She was skilled in needlework, as was her sister Martha. If it were possible to examine more closely the table coverings and cushions in the family rooms, for example, we would probably discover that many pieces were created by the two sisters.

Plate 43

Another View of Aunt Minna's Sitting Room. The furnishings of the family rooms emphasize comfort and use. There was a functional desk for letter writing and, in this photograph, we see space for books, a table to serve tea or coffee to guests, and afghans to ward off drafts.

Plate 44

Aunt Minna's Sitting Room: A Third View. The furnishings are eclectic in style: a Neoclassic chest; some exotic details in the Oriental porcelains in the glass case; a pair of late nineteenth century lamps with glass shades; genre scenes on the walls. The taste is conservative: there is little sign of interest in *Jugenstil*, the Viennese version of Art Nouveau, or in the work of contemporary Austrian painters, such men as Egon Schiele, Oscar Kokoschka, or Gustav Klimt.

Plate 45

A Corner of the Family Sitting Room. These rooms come to life in the exchange of letters between Freud and his colleague, the Swiss pastor and psychoanalyst, Oskar Pfister. On December 30, 1923, Pfister wrote, "It is now nearly fifteen years since I entered your house for the first time and quickly fell in love with your humanitarian character and the free and cheerful spirit of your whole family. The little girl [Anna] who took care of the lizards, who now writes very serious papers for the International Psycho-Analytical Association, was still in short skirts, and your second son [Oliver] played truant from school in order to introduce the boring frock-coated old pastor to the mysteries of the Prater. . . . and if I had been asked what was the most agreeable place in the world I could only have replied: 'Find out at Professor Freud's'. . . ."[38]

Freud responded a few days later, thanking Dr. Pfister for his New Year's letter and adding, with his characteristic realism, "You have the gift of throwing a rosy sheen over the everyday life one takes part in so colourlessly." He went on to thank Pfister for "saying so little about my illness, which during the past few months has been taking up too much space in our lives."[39] (Freud was, of course, referring to his struggle with cancer of the palate.)

Plate 46

The Family Sitting Room: A View from the Family Room Looking Back into Aunt Minna's Room. It was into this quiet place that the Nazi S.S. men forced their way in March 1938. Martha Freud, with her characteristic poise and restraint, had asked the men to leave their rifles in the umbrella stand in the hall and to be seated. Passports were confiscated and all the money taken from the family safe (6,000 Austrian shillings, about $840.00). Later, Freud dryly commented that he himself had never been paid so much for a single visit.[40]

Plate 47

A Corner of the Family Sitting Room. (The large photograph is of Lucy Freud, Ernst Freud's wife.) According to one report, Freud sat quietly in the armchair shown here during the Nazi raid. But he was not to be totally silenced. Before being granted permission to leave Austria, he had to sign a document saying he had been treated with respect and allowed "to live and work in full freedom" after the Anschluss. This he did, but he also asked if he could add the following sentence: "I can heartily recommend the Gestapo to anyone."[41]

Plate 48

The Dining Room. Freud, like other Viennese men of his time, always joined the family for the noon meal. He was said to be generally quiet and somewhat preoccupied at this time of day, but showed concern for the whereabouts and activities of his family. On occasion he would bring a newly purchased antiquity to the table, so he could enjoy its presence while he ate.

At times, there were visiting colleagues, "pioneers of analysis," who, according to Anna Freud, because of their "almost passionately impatient enthusiasm for science, regard[ed] time spent at the family table as an interruption of their theoretical and clinical discussions." These were exceptions though. Oskar Pfister was one guest who took a real interest in the lives of the children.[42]

Plate 49

A Corner of the Dining Room. There is a telephone on a small stand, but this was an implement Freud never enjoyed using. Another copy of the etching by Ferdinand Schmutzer hangs over the couch.

Plate 50

Family Portraits on the Wall of the Dining Room. In the top row, second from the left, is a photograph of Freud's sons, Martin, Oliver, and Ernst, in Alpine dress posed before a painted mountain scene. They appear again in the same row, though one is hidden, wearing sailor suits. And they stand (lower left) in identical jackets and caps. A picture of Martha Freud as a young mother with three of her children is at the center of the top row, and below it are two of the girls with muffs and knitted caps. Bottom right there is a picture of Freud around 1900 standing in his first consulting room, surrounded by pictures of Italy.

Plate 51

Objects in a Wall Cabinet. Surrounding miniatures of five of the children are "homely" objects: tea cozies, one, lower right, showing the spout of the teapot within; vases for flowers; glasses and compotes; a china deer; a bird. (This cabinet appears to be located in the dining room.)

Plate 52

Portrait. In May 1938, Freud, age 82 and gravely ill, was about to go into exile. Yet he was unfailingly courteous and, given his situation, astonishingly good-humored. He wrote often on man's problem in facing and dealing with death. He treated the subject poetically in "The Theme of the Three Caskets" (1913), in polemic style in "Thoughts for the Times on War and Death" (1915), again in 1915 in his papers "On Transience," in "Mourning and Melancholia" (1917), and in many others. He exhorted his readers to give up the magical denial of the finality of death, to enhance living by recognizing life's brevity, and to strive for remembrance by means of intellectual achievement.

over the years, symbols, as they were, of the discoveries and insights that had been his life's work. He was about to leave this place.

There are two letters of Freud's among the hundreds that have been preserved, that speak of leave-taking. They were written only a few years earlier to H. D. (Hilda Doolittle, the American Imagist poet who had been his patient in 1933 and 1934). He wrote the first of these just after Christmas, in 1935, to thank her for a gift. "We here, too, have more fog and darkness than is usual around Christmas time. But in front of my window in the inner room stands a proud, sweet-smelling plant. Only twice have I seen it in bloom in a garden, at the Lago di Garda and in the Val Lugano. It reminds me of those bygone days when I was still able to move about and visit the sunshine and beauty of southern nature myself. . . . It is hardly advisable to give an octogenarian something beautiful. There is too much sadness mixed in with the enjoyment.[43]

Two years before this photograph was taken, Freud wrote again to H.D., following his eightieth birthday in May, 1936, to acknowledge her expression of affection and the pleasure that her words brought him: "Life at my age is not easy, but spring is beautiful, and so is love.[44]

Plate 53

A moving photograph of Sigmund Freud at his desk surrounded by the objects he had collected

Plate 54

Freud's Appreciation to Engelman: "Heartfelt Thanks to the Artist 1938, Freud."

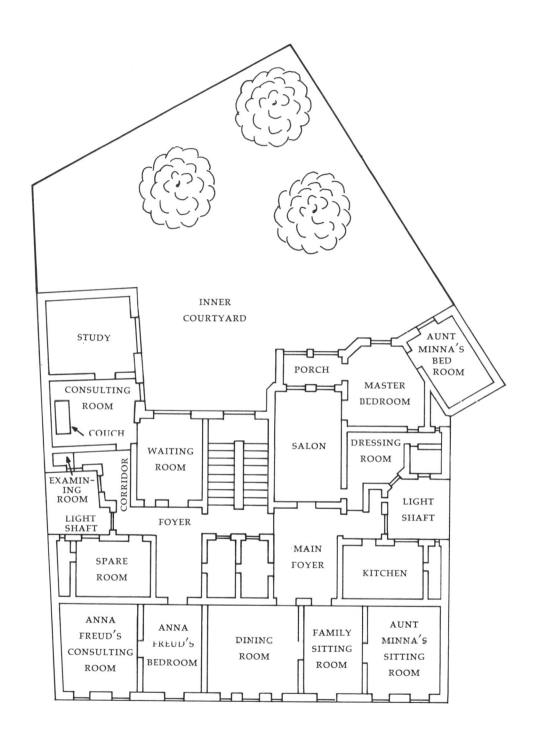

The Freud offices and family apartments
at Berggasse 19 in 1938.

THE PHOTOGRAPHS OF

BERGGASSE 19

BY EDMUND ENGELMAN

Plate 1

Plate 2

Plate 3

Plate 4

Plate 5

Plate 6

Plate 9

Plate 10

Plate 11

Plate 12

Plate 13

Plate 14

Plate 17

Plate 18

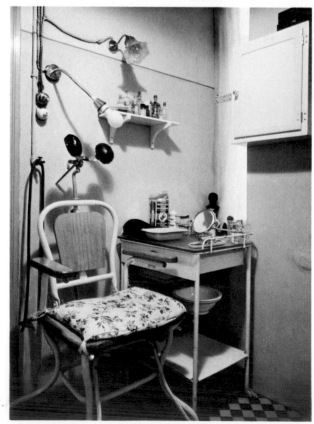

Plate 19

Plate 20

Plate 21

Plate 22

Plate 23

Plate 24

Plate 25

Plate 26

Plate 27

Plate 28

Plate 29

Plate 30

Plate 31

Plate 32

Plate 33

Plate 34

Plate 35

Plate 36

Plate 37

Plate 38

Plate 39

Plate 40

Plate 41

Plate 42

Plate 43

Plate 44

Plate 45

Plate 46

Plate 47

Plate 48

Plate 49

Plate 50

Plate 51

Plate 52

A MEMOIR

BY EDMUND ENGELMAN

IREMEMBER that I was both excited and afraid as I walked through the empty streets toward Berggasse 19 that wet May morning in 1938. I carried a little valise filled with my cameras, tripod, lenses, and film and it seemed to become heavier and heavier with every step. I was convinced that anyone who saw me would instantly know that I was on my way to the offices of Dr. Sigmund Freud—on a mission that would hardly have pleased the Nazis.

It had only recently stopped raining. The sky was still dark and the cobblestones of Berggasse were glossy and wet. The dark day worried me. I was afraid that there might not be enough light for good interior photographs of the Freud apartment. Flash and floodlights were out of the question. I had been told that the apartment was under constant surveillance by the Gestapo. The only permanent record of the place where Freud had lived and worked for the last forty years would have to be made without arousing any suspicion whatsoever. I felt fear for my own safety and also for the Freuds, for I did not want to be responsible for some misstep which would endanger them now that they were so close to leaving Vienna safely.

The idea that it would ever be necessary for the Freuds—or for me, for that matter—actually to leave Vienna had come slowly and painfully. The hatred of Jews in Vienna was nothing new to me. We had always lived with it, without a thought of ever leaving the city. It was part of Vienna, just like the Prater and the cafés—it seemed almost taken for granted, the price we paid for our pleasures. But now it was different.

The general anti-Semitism of the past had become an active, dangerous force, responsible for daily outrages and brutalities which, oddly enough, seemed at the time unpredictable and shocking.

I was born in Vienna in 1907 and grew up there. My father had emigrated as a child from eastern Europe and by his effort and ingenuity had become a comfortable middle-class businessman by the time my sister and I were in school. We lived in Leopoldstadt, a respectable but hardly affluent quarter where many Jewish families lived. Quite typically, it was my mother's major concern and hope that her children would grow up to be cultivated professionals, fully engaged in Vienna's exciting intellectual and cultural life. Most of the Viennese Jews we knew had few illusions of ever penetrating the highly stratified and intensely anti-Semitic inner circles of the city's power structure. But educational and cultural opportunities seemed to us unlimited and we strove mightily to take advantage of them.

From my earliest days, my principal interests seemed to be scientific and technical and, eager to bring out whatever talents might conceivably be lurking in their only son, my parents supplied cameras, microscopes, and whatever else their budding scholar might seem to need. When I was ten, I built my own lensless camera and proudly produced my first picture. My fascination with cameras continued to grow all through the years of my schooling, first at Real-gymnasium Leopoldstadt (which, coincidentally, was the school the young Sigmund Freud had attended years before me), and then at the Technische Hochschule of Vienna. At the "TH" I pursued a degree in mechanical and electrical engineering which, due to my growing seriousness about photography, I supplemented with studies in chemistry, cinematography, and related subjects. The "TH" was a good place to learn, but one had to be very careful there. During my years as a student, 1926–31, it was a center of intense, often violent, conservative "pan-German" political activities. Jews and other "aliens" walked carefully on campus, pitifully intent on not "causing trouble"—yet Jewish students were regularly beaten up by gangs from the nationalistic fraternities. The police, meanwhile, stood off-campus, scrupulously avoiding interference with the traditional "academic freedom" that allowed the university to pretend to be a state unto itself. My experience at the "TH" came to characterize for me the Vienna of the thirties—scientific, technical, and cultural brilliance (Ernest

Mach, Karl Doppler, and many other major figures were on the "TH" faculty) existing side by side with legalized violence.

The contrasts within the daily lives of young people like myself were, in retrospect, unbelievable. On the one hand we lived in what seemed to be an unparalleled flowering of intellect and culture. Every day we heard of new and wonderful composers, painters, films, and theories of self and society; themes and ideas that provoked long and excited conversations and debate were in the air.

But at the same time, the order provided by civil authorities eroded steadily as the government became ever more open in its attack on its enemies and less and less concerned with preserving the appearance of legal and democratic procedures. The only response available to us, such as it was, drew upon whatever cultural and intellectual skills we happened to possess—real political responses seemed hopelessly beyond us. In my case, for example, I took pictures. When the militia mercilessly shelled the *Goethehof* worker housing developments with heavy artillery in 1934 to put down an ill-equipped workers' uprising, I made a thorough photographic record of the bombed-out apartments and the homeless women and children as some kind of "evidence" (for whom, I wonder now?) of the unbelievable officially-sanctioned brutality which had taken place. (In 1938, before I fled Vienna, I destroyed the negatives of my liberal photojournalism. If the Nazis had found them, they would have been "evidence," indeed fatally incriminating evidence, against *me*.)

In 1932, in the depths of the depression, I was newly out of the university and slowly learned that I was not likely to find the position I wanted as a photographic engineer. So I opened a photographic shop called Photo City on the lively Karntnerstrasse near the Opera. It soon became well known among serious photographers as a kind of experimental laboratory and a good source of anything new and innovative in photography.

Vienna was alive with new ideas which it both pursued and resisted. One weekend in 1933, at the summer home of a friend outside Vienna, I had the pleasure of meeting a gentleman, a Mr. August Aichhorn, who was deeply involved with the highly controversial field of psychoanalysis and who, to my intense interest, was an intimate of none other than the famous Professor Freud himself. Aichhorn was respected as a teacher and a lay analyst with a special interest in psychological problems of children. Although he was not a Jew, he too had run afoul of Viennese official conservatism. He had been the founder of an innovative treatment center for juvenile delinquents near Vienna, described in his important book *Wayward Youth* (1925), which was published with an Introduction by Professor Freud. The authorities, distrusting his liberal views, closed the center.

When I met him in 1933, Aichhorn had an imposing frame, a neatly trimmed goatee, and piercing smiling eyes; he always wore a wide-rimmed black hat and was usually followed by a dachshund. Having seen him once, one could never forget him. He was a jolly person, charming and humorous, though sometimes capable of a biting wit. He never missed noticing a slip of the tongue and was always willing to supply an instructive analytical interpretation of its meaning. He enjoyed being surrounded by young people, who were fascinated by the entertaining way in which he told stories and recalled life experiences that illustrated psychoanalytic theories and demonstrated the complex workings of the mind.

Soon Aichhorn and I became cordial friends. We saw each other frequently in the years that followed, keeping in touch even during the desperate days after the *Anschluss* in March 1938 when, overnight, Austria ceased to exist and became a part of Nazi Germany. In May of that dreary spring I met Aichhorn at the Café Museum on Karlsplatz, the *Stammkaffe* where he could frequently be found. He was very upset and looked around nervously to see if we were being watched or overheard. He told me that Professor Freud, after considerable harrassment that included a Nazi break-in at his home and the detention of his daughter Anna, had finally received permission to leave Vienna for London, thanks to the intervention of high-ranking personalities and foreign diplomats. He said the Freuds would leave within ten days. The historic apartment and offices were about to be broken up for storage and shipment. It would be of utmost importance for the history of psychoanalysis, we agreed, to make an exact record of every detail of the place where it was born so that, in Aichhorn's courageous words, "a museum can be created when the storm of the years is over." I remember being impressed with his calm assumption that the thousand-year Reich would not last quite that long. In the circumstances, one wondered how he could have been so sure.

Knowing my interest and skill in photography, he asked me if I thought I could successfully take pictures of the Freud establishment and whether I would undertake to do it. I was frankly thrilled by the prospect of visiting and photographing the birthplace of psychoanalysis, of working in Freud's office and home and seeing the place where his vast output of literature was written. Above all, I looked forward to meeting Freud, who at this point in life had retired into privacy and had little contact with the outside world. Without hesitation I immediately assured Aichhorn it could be done and that I would be glad to do it. He immediately tried to dampen my enthusiasm. He suggested that I give the matter some thought. There was, he said, a good deal of possible danger. He told me that through diplomatic intervention and the payment of a ransom called *Reichs-fluchtsteuer*, or "fugitive tax," permission had been obtained for Freud and his family to leave for England and to take the contents of the office and living quarters with them. As he spoke, Aichhorn looked about him again and was careful not even to hint at the names of the people who had intervened and made Freud's escape possible. The Gestapo, he went on, warned the family not to try to bring valuables into the apartment to be smuggled out under the blanket release given for Freud's possessions. Using this pretext, the Gestapo kept a continous watch from the upper floors of Freud's apartment on the goings-on below. This was easily done because the building was U-shaped and the main rooms could be looked into from the upper floors. Any suspicious activity might attract the Gestapo's attention and lead to arrest. Aichhorn asked me if I could take these pictures without any flash or floodlight in order not to draw attention to the picture taking. I thought that I could do this, although films in those days did not have the light sensitivity of materials available today.

Still, it did not take me long to push aside the fears Aichhorn's story had provoked. After all, it was a once-in-a-lifetime chance, and I decided that nothing would hold me back from undertaking this project. Aichhorn was obviously relieved and pleased when I said so, and he then proceeded with a new warning: I should arrange my picture taking in such a manner as not to run into Freud and so disturb him. Freud, he explained to me, was already 82 years old, and had been quite ill for many years. He had contact only with his family, some of his patients, and the inner circle of which Aichhorn and Ernest Jones were members; there was also the small group that met with him weekly to play "Tarock," a card game. Aichhorn was fearful that Freud had been much upset by the intrusion of the Nazi hoodlums who had demanded and got money, and, above all, by the recent arrest of Anna who had been held by the Gestapo for several hours. Aichhorn warned me that at this time an unknown face in the apartment could create unnecessary strain for Freud.

I was somewhat disappointed to learn that I was not to meet Freud. But naturally I was excited about going ahead with the project, and I thought it would not be too difficult to arrange the picture taking without disturbing him. The apartment and offices covered a whole floor of the building and Freud, over the years, had developed a routine in the manner in which he proceeded from room to room during his day. On the basis of this routine and with a floor plan in hand, I could work out my picture-taking schedule.

The following day I met Aichhorn again, studied the floor plan, and made notes on Freud's schedule. A day later I got up early in the morning, packed my equipment— two cameras, a Rolleiflex and a Leica, with a 50mm lens and a 28mm wide-angle lens, my light meter, and as many rolls of film as I could pack into my small valise.

I decided to make my photo record as complete as possible, including the outside of the building and street. I felt that war was inevitable and that the building itself might possibly be destroyed. Berggasse, literally translated "Mountain Street," was in a middle-class, residential section of Vienna. It was cobblestoned and sloped on a hillside. The building was a massive turn-of-the-century structure with typical neighborhood stores, a butcher shop, and a food cooperative. It was a short walking distance from the University and the Psychoanalytic Institute of Vienna.

The entrance door on this day was draped with a swastika flag; another large swastika flag hung from the roof of the building. This was the way non-Jewish ownership and enthusiastic allegiance to the new regime was indicated. Freud occupied the whole second floor (which in Austria is called the first floor, or sometimes, the mezzanine). The windows of the living quarters of the Freud family faced the street. The professional offices faced the back yard. At the left, from the street, was Anna's room, then came the three windows of the dining room, and at the far right was the window to the sitting room used by Aunt Minna, Mrs. Freud's sister.

An archway led into the building. Turning right, one walked up a massive, wide

136

staircase which led to the floor occupied by Freud and his family. Aichhorn had told me that at first only half of the floor was occupied by the family and that Freud had his offices on a different floor. In 1908 he acquired the rest of the floor and moved his offices there. The landing had two doors, one to the right leading into Freud's office and another to the left, opposite, to the apartment. At the office door, I photographed the modest sign: "Prof. Dr. Freud, 3–4," his visiting hours.

I carefully photographed the street, the building, the hallway, and the staircase on which Freud had walked thousands of times, following the route taken by everyone who had ever visited there. I rang the bell and Paula, the housekeeper of the Freud family, let me in. I already had a good mental map of all the rooms and I proceeded from the foyer to photograph every detail, always keeping in mind that some day these photographs might be the only record available to recreate Freud's offices and living quarters.

In the rooms, I had intended to take as many pictures as I could from positions where Freud usually stood or sat. I wanted to see things the way Freud saw them, with his own eyes, during the long hours of his treatment sessions and as he sat writing. In practice, however, this presented problems. I couldn't, for example, fit my bulky tripod into the tight space between Freud's chair at the head of the couch and the little table covered with an oriental rug on which was set a half-dozen fragile looking Egyptian statuettes. So instead, I mixed my vantage points, often taking the point of view of a visitor to Freud, and when I could, of Freud himself.

The foyer was simple, with bars inside on the door as protection against burglary, itself not an unusual feature in middle-class Viennese homes. A right turn led into the waiting room which was simply furnished with a sofa, chairs, and a table. Framed portraits and awards hung on the wall. This waiting room, as I learned, had a very interesting history. It was the meeting room of the Psychological Wednesday Night Society. In this room distinguished members such as Adler, Steckel, Federn, and Rank met, later joined by Jung, Brill, Jones, and Abraham. But in my eagerness to get on into the "important rooms," I rushed through this one, stopping only for a quick shot of the pictures and diplomas on one wall.

To the left of the window was a large double door leading into the consulting room. I entered and had my first glance of the famous couch; it was relatively small. An-

137

tiquities filled every available spot in the room. I was overwhelmed by the masses of figurines which overflowed every surface. To the left of the door was a large bookcase covered with tall ancient statuettes. In the corner, at the end of the wall facing these statuettes, was Freud's chair, almost hidden by the head of the couch. The couch itself was covered with an Oriental rug and pillows were piled high on it, so that it seemed a patient lying on it would almost have to sit up. The walls were covered with pictures, pieces of art, mementos, and awards. At the foot of the couch was a typical Viennese ceramic tile stove. The large double door in the adjacent wall led into Freud's study. To the left and right of the door were glass showcases filled with hundreds of antiquities. These were set up in several rows; every bit of cabinet space was filled.

I had been aware of the fact that Freud was a collector of ancient art, for my closest friend was the son of a well-known antique dealer in Vienna. Once a week, Freud had made the rounds of the city's dealers. They, in turn, would know what he was looking for and saved items for him. Nevertheless, I was amazed by the unbelievable number of art objects. There was nothing of the popular Austrian Baroque or Biedermeyer art; there were only antiquities of great age—Roman, Egyptian, Assyrian, and Etruscan. Wherever one looked, there was a glimpse into the past. The view from Freud's chair, looking up at the elongated figures on the bookcase, was particularly dramatic.

Freud's consulting room had a small, almost hidden door covered with the room's wallpaper. It gave access to the outer foyer and a patient could leave Freud and the consulting room without being seen by the people in the waiting room. This door also led to Freud's personal medical treatment room which contained the chair and surgical instruments used in the frequent treatments for his cancer of the jaw.

Torn by my excitement and eagerness to look closely at every piece of art and every memento, I had to pull myself together to live up to the purpose of my visit. I carefully started to take one picture after the other in order not to miss anything, making notes in accordance with the code of each wall. I took overlapping photos of every spot of the consulting room. I had to make sure that nothing was missed. The light coming through the windows was limited. I turned on all the electric lights I could find, hoping I would not draw too much attention from curious neighbors who were above or across the courtyard, or from the more dangerous observers on the upper floors. I spent all day taking pictures, knowing I would need all of the evenings and nights for careful, but immediate, processing. Only a few more days were available and I still had the chance to reshoot photographs should any have turned out poorly. But there was very little time, and there would be no more second chances.

On the first night in my darkroom, I made a set of small proof prints and pasted them into an album intending to give them to Freud before his departure. Fortunately, all the pictures came out well, and I proceeded on the following days to pursue my room-by-room program of making a detailed photographic record.

Freud's study, adjacent to his consulting room, contained his extensive library. In it were books relating not only to his profession, but also a large collection of classic literature, including works of Goethe, Schiller, Mark Twain, Dostoevsky, and a large number of books on archeology. Photographs attached to the room's bookcases showed Lou Andreas-Salomé, Yvette Gilbert, and Princess Maria Bonaparte; there was also a photo of one of Freud's favorite dogs.

His massive desk in the study was placed between the door from the consulting room and a large window that looked out into the courtyard. Hanging from the window knob was an oddly decorative mirror. The chair, too, was quite strange. I later learned that an architect designed the chair according to instructions by Anna Freud, so that it would be as comfortable as possible for Freud to use in his favorite writing position. On the desk before the chair were tall, ancient figures placed in a row. To the right was a comfortable chair to be used by patients during initial consultations. Between the desk and the chair was a table with a large smiling Chinese figure. It struck me that Freud would have so large an object placed between himself and his patients.

The room also had showcases filled with hundreds of pieces of ancient art. Again, I recorded everything as systematically as I could, and, that night, pasted a set of proof prints into the album for Freud.

The following day, the third, while I was setting up to take some additional photos of Freud's desk (and for the first time feeling almost routine about it all), I heard short fast steps approaching. It was Freud. He had unexpectedly changed his route, returned to his study, and found me there. We stared at each other with equal astonishment. I was flustered and embarrassed. Freud looked concerned—in a calm, matter-of-fact way. I just did not know what to say to him and stood mute. Fortunately Aichhorn stepped into the room at that moment and immediately sized up the situation. He explained to Freud the purpose of my mission and introduced me. We shook hands, with evident relief. At that moment I remembered that I had the album I had prepared with me. I took it out of my valise and explained to Freud that the album was meant to be a souvenir for him to take along to England. He looked at it slowly, page by page, and picture by picture. Gradually, he began to smile—and then he smiled broadly and quite openly. Then, more seriously, he said, *"Ich danke Ihnen herzlich. Das wird für mich viel bedeuten."* ("My deepest thanks. This will mean much to me.")

I asked him whether I could take his picture. He graciously consented and invited me to proceed with my picture taking as I pleased. He then sat down in front of his desk, opened a leather folder, and began to write with a fountain pen on a large sheet of paper. At first he sat rather stiffly, looking at the camera while I prepared to take his picture, but after a few moments he turned to his desk and became so engrossed in his work that it seemed the outside world had disappeared for him. His writing, in large letters, flowed quickly and without interruption. The portraits that I took of Freud—and later of his wife and daughter—presented a special technical problem. Because of the poor light, longer exposures had to be used, but there was a danger of blurring the picture because of the movement of the subject.

During the following days it was no longer necessary to hide from Freud. I even suggested that if it would be useful and save time and trouble, I would gladly take the necessary photographs for the passport. Freud, Mrs. Freud, and Anna posed patiently. Freud, at my request, slowly turned his head, took his glasses off, and reacted with a smile to one of those remarks photographers make while trying to get ready.

Mrs. Freud, a warm, motherly woman, took me around the apartment. The living quarters had typical massive, upper middle-class furniture. The floors were covered with Oriental rugs. In contrast to Freud's professional offices, there was no ancient art. There were objects of personal nature, mementos, photographs of children, and decorative crystal and China objects. Mrs. Freud pointed proudly at some framed documents and showed me the pictures of her grandchildren. She stopped at a photograph of Albert Einstein with an inscription, and spoke with great admiration of this wonderful man.

Anna had just returned from the emigration office which had been set up at the palace of Baron Rothschild. She was somewhat agitated by the sad experience, having stood in line outside of the mansion with hundreds of frightened and depressed human beings who were subjected to indignities by Nazi officials. It was then that I made the portrait of Anna which captures, I think, the fine beauty of her sad and sensitive face during those hard days.

When I was almost finished with my work, I was asked to prepare an enlarged portrait of Freud. He signed and returned it to me, with the inscription, "*Herzlichen Dank dem Kuenstler—Freud 1938.*"

Aichhorn notified me when Freud and his family had left Vienna safely. The Austrian newspapers, to the best of my knowledge, did not take notice of this event. Not much later I started all the necessary steps to get my own passport, to secure the necessary permit to leave, and to find a country that would accept me. It was almost hopeless. In November 1938 a tragic event made conditions worse. In Paris, a desperate 17-year-old Polish refugee whose parents had been deported entered the German Embassy and shot and killed a minor consular official. This event signaled a terrible pogrom. Himmler and Heydrich organized a cruel bloodbath disguised as a "spontaneous reaction of the public" to the murder of the consular official in Paris. Thousands of hoodlums roamed the streets, smashed and looted Jewish enterprises, and attacked every Jew in sight. Thousands were deported to concentration camps. All jails were filled to capacity. There still is no record avaliable as to the number of Jews killed on November 10, 1938, the night that came to be known as "*Die Kristallnacht,*" for the glitter of the night's flying glass.

I had seen the provocative headlines of the newspapers that day and before returning home I phoned and learned that SS men had been looking for me. I decided to take a taxi, giving the driver successively various destinations, and finally ending in the crowded waiting room of a practicing Nazi lawyer. I spent the night at a friend's apartment located in the inner city, which was not a residential area. We were prepared to hide in the attic should we hear suspicious steps during the night.

The following morning I checked into a private hospital to have minor surgery performed and to stay there until the terror had somewhat subsided. When I was discharged I realized that time had run out. I had to find a way out of Austria immediately.

My immigration quota number to the United States had not come up yet and no information could be obtained as to the prospects. I had to find a different country, anywhere at all. Word had gotten around that for large illegal fees visas could be bought to South American countries. I chose this option, and managed to get a visa for Bolivia and a ticket for a boat leaving from Marseilles. Then, finally, I obtained the precious transit visa through France to rendezvous with the steamship.

On January 1, 1939 I was scheduled to leave by plane for France. All I could take along was a small valise with clothing. I thought of my precious Freud negatives, but it was far too risky to take them. Any suspicious object found at the exit control could result in detention, interrogation, and arrest. I decided to leave the negatives with August Aichhorn.

In France I met with my fiancée, who had come from Poland. We decided not to go to Bolivia after all, but to remain as illegal aliens in France until our hoped-for American immigration visas arrived. In September 1939, the long-awaited U.S. visas were issued, but just as we started our voyage, from Italy now, the war broke out and we found ourselves stranded again. Desperate weeks followed as we raced through France in search of passage, with a brief interlude in a French concentration camp as "enemy aliens." Then, finally, we found our way out and reached New York to start our new life.

As soon as was possible after the war, I began the search for my negatives, writing first to Aichhorn. Aichhorn did not live at his old address and my letter never found him. Vienna had been heavily bombed, many apartment buildings were destroyed, and it was difficult to locate anybody in the post-war confusion. When I finally learned his new address and tried to establish contact, I sadly heard that he had died. The family had given the negatives to Aichhorn's former secretary, a Miss Regele. I decided to take a trip to Europe in search of these negatives. In Vienna I learned that Miss Regele had sent them on to Anna Freud in London for safekeeping.

I traveled to London and called Anna Freud who confirmed that she had my negatives and would gladly return them to me. I went out to her house at Maresfield Gardens, gratefully picked up the negatives, and was given a tour of the house by Paula, the Freud's housekeeper whom I knew from Vienna. I was moved to see once more the beautiful pieces of art and furniture which I had last seen under such different circumstances.

The Maresfield Gardens house was beautiful, with a large wrought iron door that opened into a lush garden. Paula, still a friendly, vivacious woman, was glad to see me. She took me around and told me how happy Freud had been in this house. He would jokingly repeat a Nazi slogan—"*Wir danken unserem Fuehrer*" ("We thank our Fuehrer")—for being forced to flee Austria and find peace in this beautiful setting. He had loved the view into the backyard garden, Paula told me, and had asked to have his bed brought down from an upper room so that he could enjoy the garden view from his bed. This was where he died.

For many years, no sign existed on the house where Freud lived in Vienna. Taxi drivers who were asked by tourists to drive to the "Freud House" looked blank. In 1953 the house was finally rescued from obscurity. The World Federation for Mental Health, with permission from the Austrian government, attached a plaque to the building saying, "From 1891 to 1938, in this house, lived and worked Professor Sigmund Freud, creator and founder of Psychoanalysis." The apartment, however, remained occupied by a tenant and was not accessible to the public. In November 1969 a "Sigmund Freud-Gesellschaft" was founded in Vienna with the objective of restoring the Freud apartment and founding a museum.

I went to Vienna right after the apartment had been vacated. It was thoroughly dilapidated and common looking. I walked through the badly abused premises; little sign of their former dignity remained. The beautiful tile stoves had disappeared and had been replaced by ugly heating devices. I did not notice any major structural changes. But I was overcome by the emptiness of the rooms I walked through. Mentally, I set all the pieces of furniture in their place. I looked at the wall where the couch had been and noticed, on the wooden floor, the outline of the couch.

A week later, before leaving Vienna, I went back to Berggasse 19 once again. Workmen had already started to put the offices and apartment into shape. The floor had been scraped and polished. The ghost of the couch had disappeared.

NOTES TO THE INTRODUCTION

1. Sigmund Freud to his son Ernst, May 12, 1938, in English. *Sigmund Freud, Briefe 1873–1939*, selected and edited by Ernst L. Freud (Frankfurt am Main, S. Fischer, 1960), 435.

2. It is fair to note that for a time during the 1930s the City Council of Vienna proposed to name Berggasse after Freud, a suggestion that Freud found objectionable and that political events made impossible. And there is now a block of apartments named after Freud in the district of Vienna, the Ninth, in which he lived for so long. Ernest Jones, *The Life and Work of Sigmund Freud*, 3 vols. (New York, Basic Books, 1953–57), 2:14, 380.

3. February 1, 1900. From the German text printed in Max Schur, *Freud: Living and Dying* (1972), p. 547.

4. April 28, 1885. *Freud, Briefe*, 136. See also Jones, *Freud*, 1:xii.

5. Sigmund Freud, *The Origins of Psychoanalysis. Letters to Wilhelm Fliess, Drafts and Notes: 1887–1902*, ed. Marie Bonaparte, Anna Freud, Ernst Kris; trans. Eric Mosbacher and James Strachey (New York, Basic Books, 1954), p. 322; Sigmund Freud, *Aus den Anfängen der Psychoanalyse. Briefe an Wilhelm Fliess, Abhandlungen und Notizen aus den Jahren 1887–1902* (London, Imago Publishing Co., 1950), p. 344. [For this and other dual citations, see Bibliographical Note.]

6. Hanns Sachs, *Freud: Master and Friend* (London, Imago Publishing Co., 1945), p. 49.

7. "Reminiscences of Freud and Jung," in Benjamin Nelson, ed., *Freud and the 20th Century* (Cleveland, Meridian Books, 1957), p. 60.

8. May 8, 1901. Freud, *Origins of Psychoanalysis*, p. 330; *Aus den Anfängen*, p. 354.

9. Schur, *Freud*, p. 247. Not long after 1900, Freud publicly referred to his antiquities as a "'small collection." *The Psychopathology of Everyday Life*, in *Standard Edition of the Complete Psychological Works of Sigmund Freud*, translated under the general editorship of James Strachey in collaboration with Anna Freud, assisted by Alix Strachey and Alan Tyson, 24 vols. (London, Hogarth Press, 1953–75), 6:167 [henceforth. *S.E.*]; *Zur Psychopathologie des Alltagslebens*, in Sigmund Freud, *Gesammelte Werke*, ed. Anna Freud, E. Bibring, W. Hoffer, E. Kris, O. Isakower, in collaboration with Marie Bonaparte, 18 vols. (1940–68), 4:186 [henceforth *G.W.*].

10. February 7, 1931. *Freud, Briefe*, pp. 398–99.

11. July 17, 1899. *Origins*, p. 286; *Anfänge*, p. 305.

12. "Overdetermination" is a most useful, if perhaps infelicitously named, Freudian category. Freud first formulated it in the mid-1890s, in the years of his collaboration with Breuer, to emphasize that mental events must be traced to several regions of human psychology. The stress on the multiple causation of all events was, and remains, a salutary caution against dogmatism or reductionism.

13. January 30, 1899. *Origins*, p. 275; *Anfänge*, p. 293.

14. December 6, 1896. *Origins*, p. 181; *Anfänge*, p. 192.

15. Quoted in Jones, *Freud*, 3:83–84.

16. August 6, 1899. *Origins*, p. 291; *Anfänge*, p. 310.

17. *Studies on Hysteria, S.E.*, 2:139; *Studien über Hysterie, G.W.*, 1:201.

18. See *S.E.*, 21:69–71; *G.W.*, 14:426–27.

19. May 28, 1899. *Origins*, p. 282; *Anfänge*, p. 301.

20. December 21, 1899. *Origins*, p. 305; *Anfänge*, pp. 326–27.

21. *Fragment of an Analysis of a Case of Hysteria* ["Dora" Case], *S.E.*, 7:12; *Bruchstück einer Hysterie-Analyse, G.W.*, 5:169–70.

22. September 24, 1907. *Freud, Briefe*, p. 226.

23. May 26, 1907. Ibid., p. 251.

24. *Delusions and Dreams in Jensen's "Gradiva," S.E.*, 9:18; *Der Wahn und die Träume in W. Jensens "Gradiva," G.W.*, 8:42.

25. Quoted by Freud in *Delusions and Dreams*, p. 32; *Der Wahn*, p. 58.

26. *Delusions and Dreams*, p. 22; *Der Wahn*, p. 47.

27. *Delusions and Dreams*, p. 40; *Der Wahn*, p. 65.

28. *Delusions and Dreams*, p. 7; *Der Wahn*, p. 31.

29. Dr. Alfons Paquet, Secretary of the Goethe Prize Committee in Frankfurt, to Freud, July 26, 1930. Quoted in *G.W.*, 14:546n.

30. December 5, 1898. *Origins*, p. 270; *Anfänge*, p. 288.

31. *An Autobiographical Study, S.E.,* 20:8; *Selbstdarstellung, G.W.,* 14:34. Scholars now agree that this essay is not by Goethe at all, but by his acquaintance Christoph Tobler. See the editorial note by Andreas Speiser in *Johann Wolfgang Goethe, Gedenkausgabe der Werke, Briefe und Gespräche,* ed. Ernst Beutler, 24 vols. (Zurich, Artemis Verlag, 1949), 16:978.

32. *Studies on Hysteria, S.E.,* 2:160; *Studien über Hysterie, G.W.,* 1:227.

33. *S.E.,* 20:195; *Die Frage der Laienanalyse, G.W.,* 14:222.

34. *S.E.,* 6:101; *Zur Psychopathologie des Alltagslebens, G.W.,* 4:112.

35. Freud to Leon Steinig, June 1932. *Freud, Briefe,* p. 407.

36. *Fragment of an Analysis, S.E.,* 7:77–78; *Bruchstück einer Hysterie-Analyse, G.W.,* 5:240.

37. *Studies on Hysteria, S.E.,* 2:137; *Studien über Hysterie, G.W.,* 1:198–99.

38. *Fragment of an Analysis, S.E.,* 7:120; *Bruchstück einer Hysterie-Analyse, G.W.,* 5:284–85.

39. *Notes upon a Case of Obsessional Neurosis* [Case of the "Rat Man"], *S.E.,* 10:166–67; *Bemerkungen über einen Fall von Zwangsneurose, G.W.,* 7:392.

40. *Charcot, S.E.,* 3:11–18; *Charcot, G.W.,* 1:21–29.

41. *Fragment of an Analysis, S.E.,* 7:109; *Bruchstück einer Hysterie-Analyse, G.W.,* 5:272.

42. August 18, 1882. *Briefe,* p. 29.

43. Martin Freud, *Sigmund Freud: Man and Father* (New York, Vanguard Press, 1958), p. 43.

44. *The Aetiology of Hysteria, S.E.,* 3:199; *Zur Ätiologie der Hysterie, G.W.,* 1:435.

45. See, *The Interpretation of Dreams, S.E.,* 4:130; *Traumdeutung, G.W.,* 2–3, 136 and 136n. See also editor's note, *S.E.,* 7:128–29.

46. *The Moses of Michelangelo, S.E.,* 13:211; *Der Moses des Michelangelo, G.W.,* 10:172.

47. Heinz Hartmann, *Psychoanalysis and Moral Values* (New York, International Universities Press, 1960), p. 17.

48. July 8, 1915. Quoted in Jones, *Freud,* 2:417–18.

49. *"Civilized" Sexual Morality and Modern Nervous Illness, S.E.,* 9:191; *Die "kulturelle" Sexualmoral und die moderne Nervosität, G.W.,* 7:154.

50. April 9, 1935, in English. *Freud, Briefe,* p. 416.

51. *Fragment of an Analysis, S.E.,* 7:28; *Bruchstück einer Hysterie-Analyse, G.W.,* 5:187.

52. Hartmann, *Psychoanalysis and Moral Values,* p. 19.

53. *S.E.,* 21:144–45; *Das Unbehagen in der Kultur, G.W.,* 14:505–06.

54. March 6, 1910. *Sigmund Freud–Oskar Pfister, Briefe, 1909–1939,* ed. Ernst L. Freud and Heinrich Meng (Frankfurt am Main, S. Fischer, 1963), pp. 32–33.

55. *Dostoevsky and Parricide, S.E.,* 21:177; *Dostojewski und die Vatertötung, G.W.,* 14:399.

56. *Analysis of a Phobia in a Five-Year-Old Boy, S.E.,* 10:9; *Analyse der Phobie eines fünfjährigen Knaben, G.W.,* 7:247.

57. *An Autobiographical Study, S.E.,* 20:8; *Selbstdarstellung, G.W.,* 14:34.

58. *The Question of Lay Analysis, Postscript, S.E.,* 20:253; *Nachwort zur Diskussion über die "Frage der Laienanalyse," G.W.,* 14:289–90.

59. June 5, 1910, *Freud–Pfister, Briefe,* p. 36.

60. May 25, 1895. *Origins,* p. 119; *Anfänge,* p. 129.

61. Sachs, *Freud,* p. 70.

62. *An Autobiographical Study, Postscript, S.E.,* 20:71; *Nachschrift [Zur Selbstdarstellung], G.W.,* 16:31.

63. *Address Delivered at the Goethe House in Frankfurt, S.E.,* 21:208; *Ansprache im Frankfurter Goethe-Haus, G.W.,* 14:547.

64. July 23, 1908. *Sigmund Freud–Karl Abraham, Briefe, 1907–1926,* ed. Hilda C. Abraham and Ernst L. Freud (1965), p. 57.

65. May 10, 1926. *Briefe,* p. 365.

66. Quoted in Jones, *Freud,* 2:419.

67. September 25, 1882. *Freud, Briefe,* p. 30.

68. February 6, 1899. *Origins,* p. 276; *Anfänge,* pp. 294–95.

69. April 28, 1939. *Freud, Briefe,* p. 451.

70. *S.E.,* 21:145; *G.W.,* 14:506.

71. *Studies on Hysteria, S.E.,* 2:134n; *Studien über Hysterie, G.W.,* 1:195n.

72. May 18, 1898. From the German text in Schur, *Freud,* p. 544.

73. Ibid., p. 76.

74. May 25, 1895. *Origins,* pp. 119–20; *Anfänge,* pp. 129–30.

75. August 6, 1895. *Origins,* p. 122; *Anfänge,* p. 132.

76. *S.E.,* 4:xxvi; *G.W.,* 2–3:x.

77. *Origins,* p. 215; *Anfänge,* p. 229.

78. *On the History of the Psycho-Analytic Movement, S.E.,* 14:17; *Zur Geschichte der psychoanalytischen Bewegung, G.W.,* 10:55.

79. *An Autobiographical Study, S.E.,* 20:34; *Selbstdarstellung, G.W.,* 14:60.

80. *Origins,* pp. 218–19; *Anfänge,* p. 233.

81. *Origins,* p. 223; *Anfänge,* p. 238.

82. *Origins,* p. 233; *Anfänge,* pp. 237–38.

BIBLIOGRAPHICAL NOTE

No one who writes on Freud need start from the beginning; the literature on him is enormous and often of high quality. Few authors have been so fortunate in the editors of their collected works as he. Every student of Freud can, and must, depend on the *Standard Edition of the Complete Psychological Works of Sigmund Freud*, translated under the editorship of James Strachey in collaboration with Anna Freud, assisted by Alix Strachey and Alan Tyson, 24 vols. (1953–75). Its authority is so great that while there is a good German edition of Freud, the *Gesammelte Werke*, edited by Anna Freud, E. Bibring, W. Hoffer, E. Kris, and O. Isakower in collaboration with Marie Bonaparte, 18 vols. (1940–68), the new study edition of Freud's works that will comprise ten volumes when completed actually uses the notes of the English edition. In the preparation of this essay, I have relied on all three of these. While it is fair to say that the translators have done a heroic job rendering Freud's vigorous and supple German into English and normalizing his language across a lifetime of writing, they have often failed to convey Freud's economy of expression and to capture his felicity of formulation. Hence I have retranslated all the passages from Freud I quote and could find in German, but (both as a tribute to its excellence and a recognition of its place as indeed the standard edition) I have consulted the *Standard Edition* in making my translations. In my footnotes I cite both that edition and the *Gesammelte Werke*. This should make the work of finding any passage easy. For reasons that the editors of the *Standard Edition* have tried to explain, they have rendered some of the ordinary German words that Freud employed by more or less formidable neologisms; "cathexis" for *Besetzung* is the most notorious instance. (See *S.E.*, 3:63n.) But even the short and relatively comprehensible term *id* Latinizes the more informal German word *Es*, which is to say, plainly, "it." And there are times when the translators make Freud sound more genteel than in fact he was, rendering the blunt term *Dukatenscheisser*, which is to say "shitter of ducats," as "one who excretes ducats."

This instance of veiling Freud's direct speech occurs in the most significant collection of Freud's letters: *The Origins of Psycho-Analysis. Letters to Wilhelm Fliess, Drafts and Notes: 1887–1902*, edited by Marie Bonaparte, Anna Freud, Ernst Kris, and translated by Eric Mosbacher and James Strachey (1954). (See, for the *Dukatenscheisser* passage, p. 189.) The original version, *Aus den Anfängen der Psychoanalyse. Briefe an Wilhelm Fliess, Abhandlungen und Notizen ans den Jahren 1887–1902*, has the same editors (1950). These letters, from the critical years of Freud's conquest of the unconscious, are at once magnificent and instructive; I have drawn on them freely. There is a general selection, *Letters of Sigmund Freud, 1873–1939*, edited by Ernst L. Freud, translated by Tania and James Stern (1961), which, in view of Freud's gifts as a letter writer, could be far more comprehensive than it is without the slightest loss of interest. (The German edition is *Briefe 1873–1939*, same editor [1960].) It may be supplemented by *Psychoanalysis and Faith: The Letters of Sigmund Freud and Oskar Pfister, 1909–1939*, edited by Heinrich Meng and Ernst L. Freud, translated by Eric Mosbacher (1963); (German version, *Sigmund Freud-Oskar Pfister, Briefe, 1909–1939*, same editors [1963]), a remarkable exchange between the Jewish atheist and the psychoanalytic pastor. See also, *A Psychoanalytic Dialogue. The Letters of Sigmund Freud and Karl Abraham*, edited by Hilda C. Abraham and Ernst L. Freud, and translated by Bernard Marsh [pseud.] and Hilda C. Abraham (1965); (original version, *Sigmund Freud, Karl Abraham, Briefe 1907–1926*, same editors [1965]); *The Letters of Sigmund Freud and Arnold Zweig*, edited by Ernst L. Freud, translated by William and Elaine Robson-Scott (1970); (original version, *Briefwechsel*, same editors [1968]); and, of course, the recent *Freud-Jung Letters*, edited by William McGuire, translated by Ralph Manheim and R.F.C. Hull (1974).

Among the several biographies, the most valuable remains, with all its faults, Ernest Jones, *Sigmund Freud: Life and Work*, 3 vols. (1953–1957); though perhaps not distanced enough and often gracelessly written, it collects material not available anywhere else and offers important judgments on many aspects of Freud's private and professional life. Max Schur, *Freud: Living and Dying* (1972) is a moving and extensive biographical study from the inside; its treatment of Freud's self-analysis has been most helpful to me. It contains passages of letters to Fliess unavailable elsewhere. Martin Freud, *Sigmund Freud: Man and Father* (1958), though episodic and generally unimpressive, contains a few revealing anecdotes. H. D. [Hilda Doolittle], *Tribute to Freud* (1956) is a poetic evocation by a former patient. Hanns Sachs, *Freud: Master and Friend* (1945) is a short and wise summary by an intelligent and admiring colleague; I found myself drawing on his insistence that there was a "red thread" running through Freud's life. *Freud and the Twentieth Century*, edited by Benjamin Nelson (1957), is a mixed lot; it contains two interesting reminiscences: Abram Kardiner, "Freud—the Man I Knew, The Scientist, and His Influence," (pp. 46–58), and Viktor von Weizsäcker, "Reminiscences of Freud and Jung" (pp. 59–75).

To my mind the most rewarding short analysis of Freud's system of ideas, couched in lucid prose and presented in chronological order, is Richard Wollheim, *Freud* (1971). Philip Rieff, *Freud: The Mind of the Moralist* (rev. ed. 1961), is a substantial and thoughtful essay; I found particular use for Chapter 9, "The Ethic of Honesty." For Freud the stylist, see Walter Schönau, *Sigmund Freuds Prosa: Literarische Elemente Seines Stils* (1968), which rightly makes much of Freud's archeological analogies; and the magnificently humane "Freud als Schriftsteller," by the Swiss literary historian Walter Muschg, which hits all the right notes; conveniently accessible in Muschg, *Die Zerstörung der deutschen Literatur* (3rd ed. 1958), pp. 303–47. Suzanne Bernfeld Cassirer, "Freud and Archeology," *The American Imago* 8 (1951):107–28, adds to Schönau. Steven Marcus, "Freud and Dora," *Partisan Review* 41 (1974):12–23, 89–108, is an intelligent exploration of a celebrated Freudian case history from the standpoint of a literary critic.

For the development of Freud's ideas, see, in addition to Wollheim, cited above, Siegfried Bernfeld, "Freud's Earliest Theories and the School of Helmholtz," *Psychoanalytic Quarterly* 13 (1944):341–62, which does much to establish Freud's relations to nineteenth-century scientific ideology, and Heinz Hartmann, *Essays on Ego Psychology: Selected Problems in Psychoanalytic Theory* (1964), a distinguished collection by one of Freud's most thoughtful followers; the study most directly related to this essay is "The Development of the Ego Concept in Freud's Work," (pp. 268–96). Hartmann's long essay, *Psychoanalysis and Moral Values* (1960), a greatly expanded Freud Anniversary Lecture, boldly explores the relation of psycho-

analysis to wider philosophical issues; it eminently repays reading. I wish also to record my indebtedness to Lionel Trilling's splendid Freud Anniversary Lecture of 1955, *Freud and the Crisis of Our Culture* (1955), a lucid and courageous account of the toughness of Freud's thinking. A rather different perspective emerges from a symposium edited by Sidney Hook, *Psychoanalysis, Scientific Method and Philosophy* (1959), which subjects Freud's claims to science to rigorous, often unnecessarily hostile but sometimes rewarding, scrutiny (see especially the critical essay by Ernest Nagel, "Methodological Issues in Psychoanalytic Theory," [pp. 38–56], and the defense by Heinz Hartmann, "Psychoanalysis as a Scientific Method" [pp. 3–37]). *Sigmund Freud*, an anthology edited by Paul Roazen (1973) will introduce the reader to modern controversies over Freud, including pieces by Erich Fromm, Erik H. Erikson, Herbert Marcuse, and others. Richard Wollheim has edited a helpful anthology, *Freud: A Collection of Critical Essays* (1974), which essentially addresses itself to the relation that psychoanalysis may (or may not) have to philosophy. Fascinating insights into the development of psychoanalytic ideas are provided in *Minutes of the Vienna Psychoanalytic Society*, edited by Herman Nunberg and Ernst Federn, translated by M. Nunberg, 2 vols. (1962–70).

Freud's Vienna has not yet been completely explored. Jones's biography has much valuable material. Jonathan Miller, ed., *Freud: The Man, His World, His Influence* (1972), a series of illustrated essays, includes some helpful short pieces, notably Friedrich Heer's "Freud, the Viennese Jew" (pp. 1–20), George Rosen's "Freud and Medicine in Vienna" (pp. 21–30), and Martin Esslin's "Freud's Vienna" (pp. 41–54). Allan Janik and Stephen Toulmin provide a general, overly categorical survey in *Wittgenstein's Vienna* (1973). The book needs to be supplemented with three subtle articles by Carl E. Schorske, "Politics and the Psyche in *fin-de-siècle* Vienna: Schnitzler and Hofmannsthal," *American Historical Review* 66 (1961):930–46; "Politics and Patricide in Freud's *Interpretation of Dreams*," *American Historical Review* 78: (1973): 328–47; and "Politics in a New Key: An Austrian Triptych," *Journal of Modern History* 34 (1967):343–86. K. R. Eissler's *Sigmund Freud und die Wiener Universität* (1966) is a polemical counterattack on some of Freud's critics which sheds much light on the academic mind and anti-Semitism in Freud's time.

In conclusion I want to acknowledge personal communications from the late Heinz Hartmann, and from Anna Freud.

NOTES TO CAPTIONS

1. Hanns Sachs, *Freud: Master and Friend*, p. 50.

2. Ernest Jones, *The Life and Work of Sigmund Freud*, 3:221.

3. The Ringstrasse is the wide boulevard constructed by Emperor Franz Joseph in the middle of the nineteenth century after the fortifications that had protected the city from the Turkish invaders had been torn down.

4. Lou Andreas-Salomé, 1861–1937, was a writer and lay analyst, and a close friend of Friedrich Nietzsche and Rainer Marie Rilke, as well as of Freud.

5. Lou Andreas-Salomé, *Journal*. Quoted in *Sigmund Freud and Lou Andreas-Salomé: Letters*, p. 230.

6. Jones, *Life and Work*, 2:389-90.

7. Max Schur, *Freud: Living and Dying*, pp.247–48. See also Peter Gay's Introduction, pp. 13–54.

8. The original is in the Louvre, Paris.

9. Jones, *Life and Work*, 2:14.

10. Jack J. Spector, "Dr. Sigmund Freud, Art Collector," p. 23.

11. Sigmund Freud, *The Interpretation of Dreams*, p. 453.

12. Freud, Ibid., pp. 583 ff. See also Alexander Grinstein, *On Sigmund Freud's Dreams*, Chap. 19, and Eva M. Rosenfeld, "Dream and Vision. Some Remarks on Freud's Egyptian Bird Dream," pp. 97–105.

13. Sigmund Freud, "An Autobiographical Study," in *Standard Edition*, 20:8.

14. Freud, *The Interpretation of Dreams*, p. 584.

15. Freud's italics. Sigmund Freud, "Notes Upon a Case of Obsessional Neurosis ('The Rat Man')" in *Collected Papers*, 3:314.

16. Personal interview: Rita Ransohoff and Anna Freud at 20 Maresfield Gardens, London, May 13, 1974.

17. Freud, "Leonardo da Vinci and a Memory of His Childhood," pp. 45 ff.

18. The original painting is by Pierre Albert-Brouillet.

19. Personal communication to Ernest Jones. Quoted in Jones, *Life and Work*, 1:210.

20. Personal interview: Rita Ransohoff and Anna Freud, May 13, 1974.

21. Jones, *Life and Work*, 2:173.

22. Personal interview: Rita Ransohoff and Anna Freud, May 13, 1974.

23. According to Lady Elizabeth Naylor-Leland, Christie's Gallery, London, 1974.

24. Italics mine. Letters to Martha Bernays in *The Letters of Sigmund Freud*, p. 173.

25. According to Paula, the Viennese housekeeper, who worked for the Freuds in Vienna and accompanied them to London. She still works for Anna Freud. Spector, "Dr. Sigmund Freud, Art Collector," p. 22.

26. Anna Freud identified this urn as the one in which Freud's ashes were placed. Personal interview: Rita Ransohoff and Anna Freud, London, November 3, 1975.

27. Information on the vase came from Mark I. Davies, Director of the Center, Iconographical Lexicon of Classical Mythology, Princeton, New Jersey. Personal communications to Rita Ransohoff, December 22, 1975, January 5, 1976.

28. Personal interview: Rita Ransohoff and Felix Augenfeld, New York, October 6, 1975.

29. Harry Trosman and Roger Dennis Simmons, "The Freud Library," pp. 650, 665.

30. Jones, *Life and Work*, 3:149.

31. Anna Freud, in conversation with Erwin A. Glikes, 20 Maresfield Gardens, London, June, 1974.

32. "*Was will das Weib?*" Quoted in Jones, *Life and Work*, 2:421.

33. Personal interview: Rita Ransohoff and Robert Lustig, May 3, 1974.

34. *Introductory Guide to the Egyptian Collections in the British Museum*, p. 133.

35. Minna Bernays, Freud's sister-in-law, had left Vienna with Dorothy Burlingham on May 5. Martin, whose wife and children were already in Paris, and Freud's daughter Mathilde Hollitscher and her husband managed to leave before their parents. The words "to

die in freedom" were written in English. *Letters of Sigmund Freud*, p. 442.

36. Martin Freud, *Sigmund Freud: Man and Father*, pp. 211 ff. See also Jones, *Life and Work*, 3:219.

37. Andreas-Salomé, *Sigmund Freud and Lou Andreas-Salomé: Letters*, p. 230.

38. Oskar Pfister's correspondence with Freud began in 1909 and continued until 1937. *Psychoanalysis and Faith, the Letters of Sigmund Freud and Oskar Pfister*, p. 90.

39. *Ibid.*, p. 91.

40. Martin Freud, *Freud: Man and Father*, p. 211. See also Jones, *Life and Work*, 3:219.

41. Jones, *Ibid.*, 3:219, 226.

42. S. Freud, *Psychoanalysis and Faith*, Preface by Anna Freud.

43. H.D., *Tribute to Freud*, p. 193.

44. *Ibid.*, p. 194.

BIBLIOGRAPHY

Barea, Ilse. *Vienna*. New York: Alfred A. Knopf, 1966.

Bernfeld, Suzanne Cassirer. "Freud and Archaeology." *The American Imago*, 8 (June 1951): 107–128.

Catalogue: *Introductory Guide for the Egyptian Collections in the British Museum*. Oxford University Press, 1971.

Catalogue: *Sigmund Freud, 1856–1939*. An exhibition of the Goethe-Institut zur Pflege deutscher Sprache und Kultur im Ausland e. V., Munich. Compiled and commentated by Harold Leupold-Lowenthal, Vienna, 1972.

Freud, Martin. *Sigmund Freud: Man and Father*. New York: The Vanguard Press, 1958.

Freud, Sigmund. "An Autobiographical Study." In *Standard Edition of the Complete Psychological Works of Sigmund Freud*, vol. 20. Edited by James Strachey. London: Hogarth Press, 1925.

———. *Collected Papers*, vol. 3. Translated by Alix and James Strachey. New York: Basic Books, 1959.

———. "Leonardo da Vinci and a Memory of His Childhood" (1910). Translated by Alan Tyson. In *Standard Edition*, vol. 11. Edited by James Strachey. New York: 1964.

———. (1909) "Notes Upon A Case of Obsessional Neurosis." In *Collected Papers*, vol. 3. New York: Basic Books, 1959.

———. *The Letters of Sigmund Freud*. Edited by Ernst L. Freud. Introduction by Steven Marcus. New York: Basic Books, 1975.

———. *The Letters of Sigmund Freud and Arnold Zweig*. Edited by Ernst L. Freud. New York: Harcourt Brace and World, 1970.

———. *Psychoanalysis and Faith: The Letters of Sigmund Freud and Oskar Pfister*. Edited by Heinrich Meng and Ernst L. Freud. New York: Basic Books, 1963.

———. *Sigmund Freud and Lou Andreas-Salomé: Letters*. Edited by Ernst Pfeiffer. New York: Harcourt Brace Jovanovich, Inc., 1966.

———. *The Origins of Psychoanalysis. Sigmund Freud's Letters. Letters, Drafts and Notes to Wilhelm Fliess (1887–1902)*. Edited by Marie Bonaparte, Anna Freud, and Ernst Kris. New York: Basic Books, 1954.

———. *The Interpretation of Dreams*. Edited by James Strachey. New York: Basic Books, 1956.

———. *The Standard Edition of the Complete Psychological Works of Sigmund Freud*. Edited by James Strachey in collaboration with Anna Freud, assisted by Alex Strachey and Alan Tyson. 24 vols. London: Hogarth Press and the Institute of Psycho-Analysis, 1953–1974.

Grinstein, Alexander. *On Sigmund Freud's Dreams*. Detroit: Wayne State University Press, 1968.

H. D. (Hilda Doolittle). *Tribute to Freud*. Boston: David R. Godine, 1974.

Janik, Allan, and Toulmin, Stephen. *Wittgenstein's Vienna*. New York: Simon and Schuster, 1973.

Jones, Ernest. *The Life and Work of Sigmund Freud.* 3 vols. New York: Basic Books, 1953–1957.

Ransohoff, Rita. "Sigmund Freud: Collector of Antiquities and Student of Archaeology." *Archaeology,* 74 (April 1975): 20–26.

Rosenfeld, Eva M. "Dream and Vision. Some Remarks on Freud's Egyptian Bird Dream." *The International Journal of Psycho-Analysis* 38 (1956): 97–105.

Sachs, Hanns. *Freud: Master and Friend.* Cambridge, Mass.: Harvard University Press, 1944.

Schur, Max. *Freud: Living and Dying.* New York: International Universities Press, 1972.

Spector, Jack J. "Dr. Sigmund Freud, Art Collector." *Art News* 74: (April 1975): 20–26.

Trosman, Harry, and Simmons, Roger Dennis. "The Freud Library," *Journal of the American Psychoanalytic Association* 21:646–687.

Zweig, Stefan. *The World of Yesterday. An Autobiography.* New York: The Viking Press, 1943.

ACKNOWLEDGMENTS

I wish to thank the following authorities in the field of fine arts for their help in identifying objects in Freud's collection of antiquities: Professor Blanche Brown, Department of Fine Arts, Washington Square College of Arts and Science, New York University, New York, New York. Professor Mark Davies, Classics Department, Rutger's University; Director, The Center of Documentation, Iconographical Lexicon of Classic Mythology, Princeton, New Jersey. Richard Fazzini, Associate Curator, Department of Egyptian and Classical Art, Brooklyn Museum, New York. Virginia Field, Associate Director, and Sarah Bradley and Cecilia Levine, Staff, Asia House, New York. Professor Gunter Kopke, Department of Classical Archaeology, New York University, School of Fine Arts, New York. Marvin D. Schwartz, Lecturer, The Metropolitan Museum, New York.

I would also like to thank Ruth Blumka, whose late husband, Leopold, together with Robert Lustig and Frederick Glueckselig, were art dealers in Vienna in the 1920s and '30s, for her help. In addition I would like to thank Felix Augenfeld, George Lambert, and Lili Lobel for their personal reminiscences about Vienna. Also, Martha Bernays Randolph, Freud's niece, graciously shared her recollections of the Freud family. I am especially grateful to Anna Freud for talking with me and showing me the library, furnishings, and antiquities from Freud's study and consulting room as they have been reconstituted in her home in London.

No statement, of course, is being made on my part or on that of the consultants as to the authenticity of any of the pieces or the absolute accuracy of the identifications. Statements made on the basis of photographs alone can make no such claim.

R.R.